WHY FATHERS CRY AT NIGHT

WHY FATHERS CRY AT NIGHT

A MEMOIR IN LOVE POEMS, LETTERS, RECIPES, AND REMEMBRANCES

KWAME ALEXANDER

Little, Brown and Company
New York   Boston   London

Samayah and Nandi, this is who I am

———————

Little, Brown and Company
Hachette Book Group
1290 Avenue of the Americas, New York, NY 10104
littlebrown.com

First Edition: May 2023

Little, Brown and Company is a division of Hachette Book Group, Inc. The Little, Brown name and logo are trademarks of Hachette Book Group, Inc.

The publisher is not responsible for websites (or their content) that are not owned by the publisher.

The Hachette Speakers Bureau provides a wide range of authors for speaking events. To find out more, go to hachettespeakersbureau.com or email HachetteSpeakers@hbgusa.com.

Extract from *A Good Job* by Nikki Giovanni, p.97.
Extract from *Spin a Soft Black Song* by Nikki Giovanni, p.107

ISBN 9780316417228
Library of Congress Control Number: 2023932914

Printing 1, 2023

LSC-C

Printed in the United States of America

Versions of these poems and prose appeared in the *Los Angeles Times; Bon Appétit; Alone Together: Love, Grief, and Comfort in the Time of COVID-19* (edited by Jennifer Haupt); *Men's Health;* and *Out of Wonder: Poems Celebrating Poets* (edited by Kwame, Marjory Wentworth and Christopher Colderley).

CONTENTS

Love entered in my heart one day
A sad, unwelcome guest.
But when it begged that it might stay
I let it stay and rest
It broke my nights with sorrowing
It filled my heart with fears
And, when my soul was prone to sing,
It filled my eyes with tears.
But ... now that it has gone its way,
I miss the dear ole pain.
And, sometimes, in the night I pray
That Love might come again.

—J. California Cooper

WHY FATHERS CRY AT NIGHT

CARRYING ON

I was two. It was my birthday. She gave me wooden blocks in all shapes. For me to fit in a wooden box. A puzzle of sorts. She showed me how to do it once. Maybe twice, then said, with a smile, *Now, you figure it out, son*. I said, *Okay, Mommy*. It took a while. But I did. And, of course, I wanted to do it again and again. And she sat right there while I did. Hugging me, wiping chocolate ice cream from my lips. Telling me to be careful not to get any on my favorite black-and-white dashiki. At some point, she got up, 'cause she had to go to work, or cook, or have a life. And I was mad and sad, and unsure again. But her job was done. I'd figured that puzzle out enough times to do it by myself. And she knew that. Still, it wasn't as much fun without her. And it wasn't the same kind of happy. But I felt loved. Because she was there. And that gave me strength to carry on.

My mother died on September 1, 2017. Within a month, the cracks in my marriage emerged. They would eventually become impassable canyons. Within two years, our eldest would pack her belongings—clothes, books, heart—and leave home. And leave us. Overnight, I was barefoot on Everest. Marcus Garvey without a ship. This puzzle was now sky, the pieces of my love life scattered across it, and my mother, the one person who seemed to know how to live like a rainbow in the clouds, the woman with the answers I needed like winter needed snow, was resting in peace. And I drifted. In sadness. Seeking memory.

Barbara Elaine Johnson Alexander was my first teacher. She read to us fables and fiction after dinner. Taught us Swahili at breakfast. *Jambo* meant *Hello*. And *Kupenda* meant *to love*. I was her firstborn, full of independence and rebellion. When I didn't get my way, she would often spoil my sulking with stories that either made me howl with laughter or hang on the cliff of her tongue. I fell in love with her because of this. Because of the tender power of her voice. She made words dance off the page and into my imagination. Her morning wake-up calls were soul songs — chorus *and* verse. She called us for dinner like we'd won something. A nighttime poem became a play became a production that me and my sisters embraced. Our bedrooms were Broadway. She taught me an appreciation of language by reciting Lucille Clifton and Nikki Giovanni aloud. She showed me rhythm and melody when she turned off the television, to our dismay, and sang African folktales, like "The Beautiful Girl Who Had No Teeth," which Eartha Kitt made famous. And no matter how many times I wanted to hear Dr. Seuss's *Fox in Socks*, she let me hear it. When I could read on my own, she listened to me. Over and over. She helped me to love each day with words. And that gave me courage.

When I was three, I went to a school in Morningside Heights, at 490 Riverside Drive. It was housed in Riverside Church, a progressive, interdenominational, interracial, and international church near Columbia University — where my parents were enrolled in graduate school. One day, as a tribute to my mother, I built a magical castle out of wooden blocks. It housed the ideas galloping through my creative mind, and I couldn't wait to show her. Until a contumelious classmate knocked my blocks down. It was the end of the day and his excuse was *Playtime is over. Time to clean up.* I protested. Defended myself with the only weapons I had, words: *Those were my blocks that you knocked. Lest you want a quick pay-back, better fix my quick-block stack.* Surprisingly, the boy started crying. Now, I don't remember any of this, but my mother said that when she came to pick me up that day, the teacher told her, *Your son intimidates the other children with his words. He is a little arrogant.* At this point in my mother's recounting, you could see the universe of pride and love entering her heart. "I smiled and told your teacher, *Thank you. We teach him to use his words.*

This is not a traditional memoir. Is not me climbing the stairs of yesterday and telling of each journey, step by step. Is not me gathering together all the things that have made a life out of me. Is not me opening a door to my mother's death or my father's life so that I can understand my fate as a man. As a father. As a son. These are just snapshots of a man learning to love. Again. This is a window into the darkness of doubt and the unbearable lightness of being in love. Remembrances of a poet grappling with loss and longing. Questions he's been too afraid to answer. This is a putting back together. A carrying on. A boy sealing his familial cracks, repairing romance, building a monument of love with the only tools he has.

His words.

A LETTER TO MY DAUGHTERS

Ever since I was a child and discovered his framed "Marriage Counselor Accreditation Certificate" tucked inside a *Sexual Intimacy in Marriage* manual in our garage, I have wanted to speak to my father about marriage. Now, as an adult, I wonder did he and my mother ever hold hands. How did he court her? Did he dance with her and then help her with the dishes? Did he make love to her in the kitchen? Did she rub his scalp after? How did they love is the question I've contemplated asking during those times when my own love life was discomfiting or in peril. I've wanted to know more about the woman he had a child with, the woman who was not my mother, his wife. I've wanted to ask him did he love her, too. When my mother, fed up, finally moved out, was their marriage better? Did she date, did he? Why didn't they ever divorce? As I stand on the ledge of the unraveling of my own coupling I have so many questions for the man who made me, but I'm too afraid to ask.

This book began as a collection of love poems. But somewhere along the way, I began pondering why I was writing about the thrill of a red-hot glance on a spring afternoon, or the parting of butterscotch lips, or the irrepressible hopelessness of losing a lover. Because I wanted to and I could were not good-enough answers. The art, you see, cannot be just for the sake of the art. There must be a greater good, something meaningful, something significant. And that led me here to both of you, the two greatest loves of my life. The daughters I've cherished... and let down... and hoped to one day find the courage to tell about what I know about how to love... and what I don't— which is a lot. All the things I wished I could have learned from my mother and was too afraid to ask my father are between these covers. Think of this as less a rule book on romance, more a testimony of devotion and dolor... The way I love is not on trial here, but if it were, this would be my opening statement and closing argument. Which, of course, means you would be the judges. Caution: The poems and letters and thoughts here will not tell you that I have it all figured out (I sure as hell haven't), but they will show you how much I've enjoyed the trying. And they will explore the moments of disappointment that have shaped me, and how each failure has nearly destroyed me. And they will reveal my discovering that I didn't need to understand love, I just needed to believe in it. This is all to say that I just want you to know how I have loved so that you may know what it looks like, so that you can believe in it too.

HOW TO READ THIS BOOK

Start with a chamomile
or Darjeeling black
in a clawfoot bathtub (or a wicker chaise,
on a patio)
a plate of warm scones
fresh strawberries that taste
like an unexpected kiss.

Remember the ordinary things:
a hug before the first day of school
the holding of a hand at a pep rally
making a lover laugh
in church.
Sing along if you recognize
the sacred music
between each line.

Let your fingers turn
the pages of your precious life.
Like me, be afraid of what you find:
the discovery of audacious passion
its trembling fire that melts
the recklessness that burns
the fiery footprint it leaves.

Let these humble meditations and musings
carry you close, permanent, abreast—a wave.
Go, raise a toast.
Sip.
Swallow
all the words
that hold you
hopefully inspiring
a sea of new ones.
Now, trust your heart
and the ocean of sweet possibility
brewing inside.

PART ONE

LOOKING FOR ME

What you help a child to love can be
more important than what you help them to learn.

—African proverb

PORTRAIT OF NEWLYWEDS: 1967

West Side Chicago. Sitting
on Uncle Robert's front porch.

Boxwoods and thick evergreen shrubs
on either side.

In the middle of the night
and the Six-Day War

he decided to drive through the night
in their brand-new green Ford Fairlane 500

with no air conditioning.
Only stopping once

at a truck stop for gas and cashews
and a quick nap

because it is a thirteen-hour drive
from W. 122nd and Amsterdam.

She is smiling. Politely.
He looks amused, his head tilted

like he's just made a wisecrack.
Black tube socks pulled nearly to his knees,

his highwater khakis are wrinkled
like he pulled them out of a hamper.

Her hair is primped, nails polished
like she is headed to a ball.

They are not a year married
I am twelve months away

and I notice everything
especially the way they aren't holding hands

and are sitting three feet apart
a world of trouble between them

as if earlier they'd had an argument
about an old girlfriend who'd called him

and he said she was talking stupid
so she refused to iron his pants

and stormed out of the guest room
then after breakfast, right before her husband left

to deliver the day's mail
Aunt Ethel asked if she could take a picture

of the newlyweds.
So here they sit

on the top step
like two perfectly pruned plants

in early summer
posing in love.

THE HEAVY WEIGHT OF FATHERHOOD

My father sometimes loved us
like a boxer

would tag us with biting gibes
when he was too busy
to answer a question

throw numbing jabs
that stabbed our ears
and growing hearts
when he was upset

Round after round
my mother would referee
but he would back even her into the ropes.
The man would not stop
until he knocked us all down.
Then, when he was satisfied
that we were down for the count —

(My sisters emptied of joy.
Me, defeated and repressed)

—he'd retreat to the corner
and massage our wounds
with a softening tongue
an honest humor
a familial allegiance
that lifted us all up
that left us each smiling
and revived
and almost forgetting
the sting
of his love.

THE GOSPEL TRUTH

Kneeling in the musty attic
looking for our old record player
inside cobwebbed milk crates
filled with moldy textbooks, dissertations
and his old, fiery sermons on cassette
next to a green milk crate of expired passports and
    credit cards
I discover jazz
for the first time—Duke Ellington's "Heaven"
nestled right between Nancy Wilson
and Miles Davis
the three of them side by side
trumpeting a kind of sentimental wonder.
It is up here in this sacred space
where I find the melody to build a dream on
where I rejoice
where I realize
he may not be All Blues
where I fall in love
with my father.

A LETTER TO MY FATHER

Jazz is the way brown sugar would sound if it was
   sprinkled in your ear.

—DJ Renegade

When I write, I listen to jazz music. Mostly, Bebop and Hard
Bop because of the soulful rhythm and tempo. It's dance-like,
but not dance. There are no words to distract me, and it's just
enough groove to keep my head nodding, my butt in the chair,
and my pen moving to the blazing melody. While I was writing
The Crossover, I happened upon an album by jazz pianist Hor-
ace Silver called *Song for My Father.* This was apropos because
when I think about that novel, it was a song for you. A letter of
hope for us. An inadvertent plea for you to be proud of me. Let
me explain.

Memory can be harsh. Unforgiving. When I look back on
my childhood and young adulthood, I do not remember hot
dogs and soda pop summers. My tongue was never sweet on
cotton candy because there were no moonlit carnivals. I remem-
ber craving your touch, some small ritual of precious contact,
like a drop of water in noonday heat. Time was money, smiles

were seldom, our home was serious business—book publishing—with little time for little things like card games or Ping-Pong or talking. Your conversations were instructions: *Mow the lawn like this, rake the leaves like that, and when orders come in, make sure you take down the message verbatim.* When you travelled to some church to preach about *Black Liberation Theology,* or some conference to speak about *Teaching the Culturally-Particular African American Child,* I'd simultaneously miss my father *and* feel rescued from the prison of words you kept me in.

You see, growing up, I don't recall seeing you without a book in your hand—at the dinner table, watching PBS, on your way to the bathroom. I still have this image of you sitting in your favorite chair in the family room, the evening news on, and you writing a sermon or editing a column. Books were your best friends, and you tried to make them mine. *Read the dictionary. Read the encyclopedia. Read the dissertations.* There's a friend of mine named Penny Kittle who runs an organization called BookLove and as much as I love and support the important work she is doing, the twelve-year-old in me cringes when I see those words together because it was not that.

You were driving us to our family's annual African Heritage Book Fair in Harlem, to host workshops and panels, and to sell books—many of which I'd become familiar with because you'd made me read them—*The Wretched of the Earth* by Frantz Fanon, the Heinemann *African Writer Series, Crisis in Black Sexual Politics* by Nathan and Julia Hare, Lucille Clifton's latest poetry collection, *Mufaro's Beautiful Daughters* by John Steptoe. It didn't take fourteen-year-old me long to realize

I could simply read the jacket, the introduction, and the last chapter of some of the less interesting books—*The Egyptian Book of the Dead*—and know enough to recommend it to a customer (or respond to your impromptu quizzes). The last thing I remember is being hungry and asking when were we going to eat, and being ignored, and you talking to Mommy about one of the speakers cancelling at the last minute and her assuaging your frustration with her plan to do a second African folktales reading. And, then I fell asleep. And you did too. At the wheel of the red Mercury Thunderbird. The car flipped over a dozen times, and we landed upside down. In the middle of the New Jersey Turnpike. You roll-called and checked to make sure everyone was okay. When you got to me, I was simply proclaiming what everyone was thinking, when I uttered *Dayum*. The next words out of your mouth pretty much summed up my childhood: *KWAME, WATCH YOUR WORDS. Now crawl out and get all the books.* We'd just been in a major accident and your concern was that I not curse, and that I somehow get out of the overturned car and gather the books from the trunk that were now strewn out all over the turnpike. But, here's the thing, nothing about that exchange, or your instructions, seemed strange. This is how we were. Who we were.

We made it to the bookfair, and people came, and we sold books, and we laughed, and we ate (never behind the book table, because it wasn't professional), and went on about our family business, never speaking a word about the accident on the Turnpike that left me bruised, outside. And a little on the inside.

You've heard me speak about the tyrannical state with

which you led our household. You've read about my complaints growing up under the rule of such a stern, bookish father. And no doubt, the words in these pages will reveal how I saw you and Mommy love. Or what I didn't see, and how that has impacted me. Memory can be hard. But, when you really peel away its tough skin, you begin to see the layers to love.

After college, when I wanted you to publish my first poetry book, you said *No,* that poetry would never sell. When I told you I had started my own publishing company, and that I needed seventeen hundred dollars to get my first book back from the printer, you lectured me on making bad decisions then wrote me a check for seventeen hundred dollars. As an adult, we talked maybe once every month or two. Our phone conversations consisted of you telling me everything I was doing wrong, me growing angrier and more eager to hang up. And then came *The Crossover.*

The first call I made after winning the Newbery Medal for the Most Distinguished Contribution to American Literature for Children was to Mommy. But, she didn't pick up. So, I woke you up, and when I told you, your response was simply, *Yeah, we did it!* And, then you proceeded to call me every day. And we talked. Like old friends. No more scolding lectures, scalding hot arguments that burned. Ours became full of light shining; a new world. You made jokes, I laughed. I talked with authority. You listened. We did this every day. For hours, it seemed. You even ended one of our late afternoon chats, with a matter-of-fact *I love you,* and I remember thinking how odd it sounded rolling off your tongue, but how good it felt hearing it.

I remember Mommy calling me one day and asking why the two of us were talking so much, and it was the first time I'd ever heard jealousy in her voice. And then she heard my happiness. That I'd finally understood why she stayed with him, even after she left. That you do love. In your very own special way.

Once, Mommy asked me why I wrote so many poems about you, and never wrote poems about her. I tried to explain that poets, like comedians, rarely speak about the things and people who make them happy, only the ones who cause us heartache and misery. She laughed at that. Even though I know you loved us, me, when I think back on childhood, there was one specific, reoccurring moment that made it clear and concrete for me. Every Sunday, when your sermon ended, and the pews emptied, you would come down out of the pulpit, and I would meet you at the front of the congregation. As you shook hands with each of the congregants, I would shadow your stillness, hoping for some movement on this desert island. I would look up at you, the sweat clinging from your high mountain. Your face would be a golden moon, and your hands, spring rain drizzling scalp. You rubbing the top of my head every Sunday made everything perfect, even when it wasn't. Made up for all the tyranny (Okay, so that's the twelve-year-old me talking). That's how I knew.

Look, we may have never played enough Ping-Pong together. I may have wondered why I never saw you hold Mommy's hand. You may have spent Saturday night writing a sermon instead of playing Monopoly with us. But, when I peel back the layers, I see that we each love in different ways. And, the whole time I was wondering how you loved, you were showing me the way you love. You were teaching me something about love. Something big. You taught me how to love *words*. And words taught me how to find my voice. And lifting my voice has taught me how to love the world. And, oh yes, *What a Wonderful World* that is, Daddy. Thank you!

PORTRAIT OF A TWELVE-YEAR-OLD BOY

At Vacation Bible School
a girl named Francine liked me
but I kept calling her 'Black Knees'
because hers were dark and ashy
like she'd painted them with chalk
and because I didn't want Myra
the girl whose bouncy lips
had the softness of grapes crushed by rainfall
to think I did not like her.

Myra had the kind of billowing walk
that let me know I was in over my head
but I was too caught up in her sway
too distracted by the movement of her mouth
during choir rehearsal
to realize I was in over my head.
When I called her and asked if I could be her boyfriend
she agreed, told me if I came over
she would teach me a few things.

Too afraid for the lesson she promised
I stayed away most of that summer.
Cedric had laughed at me, echoed
my belief that she was out of my league
said I should just stick to reading those books
about love in my father's garage
because that was the closest I'd ever get to third base.

When I finally got up enough nerve
to walk up to Myra's front door
I was stunned to find my best friend, David,
in his matching peach khakis and Saddlebred polo
taking her class, standing there on her porch
like a pitcher on the mound
ready to strike.

The next Sunday I saw Francine
at church and we shared
a hymnal
during the service
and I realized how pleasant
her voice actually was, how each note she sang
was a beautiful raindrop,
a black pearl plucked from
a crown of joy.

When I asked her if I could come over
to her house to maybe hang out
she looked into my eyes, unflinchingly,
for the entire second verse of "Amazing Grace,"
and I found in hers, my reflection—lost
and lonely—long after she'd rolled her eyes
and turned away.

GOLDEN TIME

Every now and then I will be
in the kitchen alone, squeezing
a lemon into milk, melting butter, or pinching
salt: and a song will come on—Let's say
a Frankie Beverly—and my shoulders will start rising
and spilling like a small wave *Running*
Away, like the tender heart of a *Southern Girl*,
and my palms will get all sweaty, and I'll whip
my head, like the eggs, back and forth,
the smile across my face swelling with each seducing
melody, and I'll forget what's in the oven
and remember how my cousins and I would lay
back in the shade at family reunions lunching
on barbecue chicken and *7Up* pound cake listening
to the laid-back groove, spellbound, watching how
Uncle Richard and his boyfriends would bend
sprightly toward the dance floor, burn
it all the way up, then thrust themselves
into each other like two souls on fire with

such unadulterated joy that everyone was
always happy and full
on love.

7UP POUND CAKE

7Up pound cake is an old-fashioned southern dessert that's just about perfect after a great meal or at a cookout (or on Sunday morning, after a long Saturday night, with a cup of English Breakfast tea). This smooth, buttery pound cake is made from scratch with just the perfect hint of that lemon-lime. You can eat this cake without any icing, it is just so incredibly flavorful, sweet, and moist (most of the time). On top of being delicious, this 7UP pound cake represents family tradition, connection, and love. (Now, for the best results, don't go substituting Sprite, or any other soda for that matter.) I make this for dinner parties with my writers' group, or Sunday dinners. (It usually lasts a little under a week.) What I'm listening to while I bake: "Moody's Mood" by George Benson.

TOTAL TIME: 1¼ HOURS

MAKES: 16 SERVINGS (OR 8 BIG ONES)

CALORIES PER SERVING: 470

COURSE: DESSERT

Ingredients

1 cup (2 sticks) unsalted butter, softened

2½ cups sugar

5 large eggs (room temperature)

3½ cups all-purpose flour

2 teaspoons baking powder

Pinch salt

½ cup milk

½ cup 7Up

2 teaspoons vanilla extract

Instructions

Preheat the oven to 350 degrees.

Grease and flour a 12-cup Bundt cake pan, shaking out excess flour.

In a large mixing bowl, blend the butter and sugar until fluffy, whipping in the sugar a little at a time. Add the eggs one at a time. Sift the flour and baking powder together with a pinch of salt. Starting and ending with the flour mixture, alternately add the flour mixture and the milk to the butter and sugar mixture, then add the 7UP. Add the vanilla. Spoon the batter evenly into the pan. Bake for 55 minutes to an hour, until a cake tester comes out clean or with a few crumbs adhering to it.

A RECIPE FOR LOVE

The people who give you their food give you their
heart.

—Cesar Chavez

There's this scene in the film *Like Water for Chocolate* where
Tita prepares quail in a rose-petal sauce from a rose given to
her secretly by Pedro. In the first ten seconds of the scene, no
one is talking. They're just eating and being overwhelmed by
desire. The meal serves as an aphrodisiac for the whole family,
especially Tita's sister, who, get this, proceeds to undress at the
table. The edacious desire in this scene, and throughout the
movie, is triggered by a plethora of elaborate dishes. Quite
beautifully, cooking and eating are out-of-body experiences in
this story, as they can be in life. I know this firsthand.

From the second we are born, the experience with food is
connected to being held, the warmth of our mother's skin, her
soothing voice. Scientists say that all these experiences are
encoded in our infant nervous system as a single event of idyllic
tenderness. Later, as adults, the ritual of breaking bread around
a table is how we share the things that matter most with the

people who matter most to us. I fell hard in love with both of your mothers over a homemade meal. Since I was a child, I've known, felt intrinsically, the relationship between love and happiness. Here's where that started.

On Saturdays during the summer, my mother would drop me off at her mother's house. Upon arrival, I'd wave goodbye to my mom, hug Nana, grab whatever cold drink was at the top of her cooler—she kept cans of ginger ale, grape soda, and root beer not in her always-packed fridge, but rather in a cooler on the floor in her petite dining room, and since we weren't allowed to drink sodas at home, well, I'd struck gold—then head to Barraud Park, which was originally land owned by the Barraud family, French Huguenots from England, until they sold it to the city of Norfolk, Virginia, to be used as the first recreational area for Blacks. My walk was a winding half-mile journey past single-family homes, through housing project courtyards. I'd spend most of the late morning and afternoon playing tennis at the park with other players, some youths, others mostly adults, in the American Tennis Association—known as the ATA, a national organization of Black players founded nearly a hundred years ago that produced legends like Althea Gibson and Arthur Ashe. The walk home was always joyous and exciting, whether I won or lost my matches, because I knew when I set foot in her driveway, a pitcher of lemonade and a glass of ice would be waiting on a table on the front porch. And so would my granddaddy.

After a few minutes of me recounting the number of aces I served, or forehand winners, he would notice a dangling gutter and proceed to curse at it, or a friend of his would stop by and he'd greet them with loving profanity, or he'd start cussing out the dog, Boomer, for barking too much. I found this random vulgarity unsettling and hilarious. Holding my laughter in until he was far away from the porch, this was my cue to come inside. To the kitchen.

Nana didn't cook on Saturdays, unless there was a spades or dominoes party at her house Saturday night, which when I think about it was every Saturday. But during my afternoon visits, she'd warm up leftovers for me. And she didn't have a microwave, so my post-tennis meal was always readied in a huge black cast-iron skillet. There were always options on what I could have, mostly seafood, but every now and then she'd have leftover turkey legs with egg noodles. Here's how it went down: She'd boil the noodles al dente, then place them in a glass baking dish with seasoned turkey legs and bake for nearly two hours, until the meat was falling off the bone as easily as autumn leaves from the yellow poplar tree in their front yard. To heat them up, she put a little butter in a pan, then when it sizzled, she dropped a heaping spoonful of turkey and noodles in the pan and let it fry. She placed a plate and a loaf of white bread (because she knew how I felt about bread) in front of me, then sat down at the opposite end of the table. We chopped it up for the next hour or so while I feasted, first with a sterling silver fork, then my savory fingers. We talked about how I was doing in school, what books my father was making me read this week, which girl was breaking my heart. We would always conclude the meal with her sharing stories about my mother as a well-behaved child, I guess to inspire me to stop acting up in church or stop picking on my sisters or whatever wrongheadedness her daughter had shared with her about me that week. It didn't work.

But our time together was special, in that she listened to me when other adults didn't seem to. She sang to me. Let me roam and rummage through her antique-filled attic when I asked. Was just a kind and sweet woman who happened to be my grandmother. We laughed a lot together, mostly at my grandfather, who would march in the house asking her *Why you letting that boy eat up all my good food?* She'd rub his head and tell him *Sit down, so I can make you a plate.* I loved how he recognized her food as *good*. And I loved how she rubbed his head. There was a fifty-year love affair that I never took for granted, never understood, and always, always appreciated.

My father's mother, Granny, made dinner, for thirty-plus folks—children, grandchildren, neighbors, siblings—every Sunday. How she cooked so much food and still made it to church early to take her seat as head of the usher board, I will never comprehend. But she climbed that mountain every week, and when we'd come by around nine in the morning to pick her up, I'd always volunteer to go in and get her.

Her house, which she and my grandfather built—during which process she'd lost a thumb—was a cornerstone of the community. The two-story Colonial featured a large green "A" on the front shingle. When I'd open the door, she'd be sitting on her screened-in porch, rocking back and forth and drinking a bottle of Pepsi. Once, when I was alone in her kitchen, I'd snuck a swig of the remains of her opened soda bottle and inadvertently downed what I recall being snuff. To this day, I can't drink Pepsi. When I think back on it, it feels like Granny was ten feet tall in that rocking chair. I can't recall how tall she was, but her son was six foot three, and I'm an inch taller, so she must have been tall, or had a tall presence. I'd give her a kiss on the cheek and not dare tell her that it was time to go, because you don't rush a seventy-year-old woman who's ten feet tall, especially one who makes the best homemade rolls this side of heaven.

In greeting me, she'd say my name like it was a question, like she was challenging me to remember who I was, and whose I was. Then she'd ask me about my grades, and scream at her husband *Come on, Tilt!* His middle name was Tilton. Finally, when he continued to ignore her after her third summons, which I was certain people a mile away could hear, she'd send me in to get him. On my way upstairs to his bedroom—they slept in separate quarters for as long as I knew them, which never seemed an abnormal thing to me—I'd detour to the kitchen with one single, precious purpose in mind. To see the yeast dinner rolls rising, to smell the sweet paradise living in nearly a dozen tin and aluminum pans.

After church, every family member and friend—most invited, some not—raced to her house for fried chicken, collard greens, potato salad, candied yams, and hot rolls with butter cuddling inside and out. There was always a battle for her rolls, the perfect blend of soft and sweet. Most people were happy to get one, lucky to get two, and very rarely got to three. But I did. Always. You see, every Sunday, your great-grandmother, the woman who always smiled at me even when I was acting up, the woman who loved singing gospel songs while she cooked (and she couldn't sing a lick), the woman who made food for a whole community and didn't eat until everyone was served, would make a special pan of four, sometimes five rolls. For me. I never had to fight for paradise, because I had my own. This woman loved me, and no matter how many times she'd spanked me with a bristly switch from her pine tree, and it was a lot, I loved her. And her rolls.

Nandi, your mother and I went to Pizza Inn on our first date. We were broke college students at Virginia Tech, and their lunch buffet was $4.99. I knew she was worthy of at least a sandwich and fries from the deli, Macados, but I couldn't afford that. So, in between slices of cheese and pineapple and pepperoni, I recited to her love poems . . .

Lips like yours
ought to be worshipped.
See, I ain't never been too religious
but you can baptize me
anytime.

For our second date, I invited her over for dinner. I prepared baked fish, rice with vegetables, and hot buttered rolls. Now, I couldn't cook, at all, but I put a lot of love into the effort, and I think she recognized that. A day before, I'd used half of my work-study paycheck to make a long-distance call to my aunt Barbara to ask her for Granny's recipe. She laughed and said, *She didn't write it down. It was just a little bit of this and a little bit of that.* I know the rolls were a little hard, and not as sweet as Granny's, but your mother never said a word. She just kissed me. And we listened to jazz records I'd "borrowed" from my father, and . . . this is the part that you probably want to skip over, maybe, my dear . . . we made love. We made you (Okay, not that day, but not too soon after).

Samayah, your mother and I were best friends for years, long before the lighting of any romantic flame. We regularly went to the movies with a group of friends, we talked about our relationships, we may even have double-dated with our significant others. We were platonic in our love for each other until 1994 when the Knicks lost to the Houston Rockets in the NBA play-offs.

We were talking on the phone like we always did, laughing about something that happened in a *Frasier* episode, discussing my latest poem, or maybe planning a skiing trip with our friends, when I invited her over for dinner. Not as a date, but as a way to help save her wallet. You see, when you opened her refrigerator an avalanche of Styrofoam containers occurred. She ate out all the time. She agreed to come over for a meal, and I went out shopping for the goods.

I cooked jasmine rice and mock duck, which was this fake duck, not real duck, I'd bought from the Seventh-Day Adventist Store in Takoma Park. I didn't know whether she'd like it, so I also made something I knew she would like. Baked turkey and noodles. My mother had given me her mother's recipe, and when I saw the juicy meat falling off the bones, I knew I'd followed it right. The game started at eight o'clock, the same time I'd set dinner. By halftime, she hadn't shown up. This was maybe a few years before cell phones became available. At the end of the game, I was pissed off that Patrick Ewing and the Knicks had lost, and I was concerned that my best friend hadn't shown up. Was she okay? When she finally called, at close to eleven o'clock, and told me she'd forgotten about the invitation, I was livid. She said she'd been getting her hair done, and I blurted out *Hair today, gone tomorrow.* Later, hours after we hung up and I'd styrofoamed the leftovers and placed them in *my* fridge, I lay in my bed sad, and happy, and no longer confused as to why. I was in love. With my best friend.

> Sometimes I wish we weren't friends
> then i could look into your bold eyes
> and find answers to questions i'm afraid to ask
> but for now, i'll stick to quick glances
> and other friendly gestures...

Food is something that we pass down from one generation to the next. The cooking of it, the sharing, the conversations over it, our hopes and plans. We put these things on a plate, serve them to the people who carry our hearts in theirs, and it makes us happy. Because it makes them happy. This is why I love to cook. It's the legacy of love that I've been gifted, that has shaped the lover in me, that has created the greatest loves of my life. You. What my grandmothers gave me, I now offer to you. A recipe for love. Won't you come on in my kitchen.

GRANNY'S HOT BUTTERED ROLLS

I reverse engineered my memory of Granny's rolls, and this is the closest I've ever come...
What I'm listening to while I bake: "Brighter Day" by Kirk Franklin.

TOTAL TIME: 6½ HOURS

MAKES: 16 TO 24 ROLLS

CALORIES PER SERVING: 140

COURSE: DINNER

Ingredients

1 package active dry yeast	1 teaspoon salt
¼ cup warm (not hot) water	1 cup warm (not hot) milk
2 large eggs	4 cups all-purpose flour
½ cup sugar	Shortening
⅔ cup unsalted butter, softened	

Instructions

Dissolve the yeast in the warm water and set aside. Beat the eggs and sugar together, then add ⅓ cup butter. Add the salt and the warm milk to the egg mixture. Next, add the dissolved yeast and the flour and mix well. Turn dough onto lightly floured surface. Knead about 5 minutes or until smooth and elastic. Place the dough in a greased bowl and cover with a damp dish towel. Set in a warm place for five hours or more for the dough to rise, at least double the size. (You can also heat the oven to 175, then turn it off, and place the dough in the oven with the door cracked open.)

Punch down dough. Thoroughly grease your round pan or baking dish with shortening. Melt the remaining butter with a tablespoon of shortening. Use this mixture to grease your hands, then divide dough into 15-20 pieces and roll to form balls. Place the rolls about ¼ inch apart in the baking dish, coat with butter/shortening mixture, cover, and let rise for another hour or so.

When the rolls are almost doubled in size, preheat the oven to 375 degrees.

Bake for 12 to 18 minutes, until the tops are golden brown.

TURKEY LEGS WITH NOODLES

——

My mother, whose turkey legs tasted even better than Nana's, gave me the recipe, but I lost it. And my sisters, who cook way better than me, don't write anything down either. So this is me trying to piece together all the things Nana and Mommy did to make this the meal I loved the most. I added the carrots because you at least need the pretense of a good meal that is somewhat good for you, right?

What I'm listening to while I bake: "Something About You" by VINX.

TOTAL TIME: 1¾ HOURS

MAKES: 6 TO 8 SERVINGS

CALORIES PER SERVING: 750

COURSE: DINNER

Ingredients

8 ounces egg noodles

4 turkey legs

¼ cup (½ stick) butter, softened

Salt and pepper to taste

1 tablespoon poultry seasoning

2 tablespoons onion powder

2 tablespoons paprika

½ cup water

2 carrots, medium diced

Instructions

Cook the noodles about half of the recommended time so they are al dente.

Preheat the oven to 350 degrees.

Rinse and dry the turkey legs. Slice deep into the tissue three times. Rub with the butter, then sprinkle salt and pepper and poultry seasoning under and over the skin. Generously season with the paprika and onion powder. Pour the water into a glass baking dish or roasting pan and add the turkey legs, noodles, and carrots.

Bake uncovered for 1½ to 2 hours, until the legs are bronze. Add more water if needed and baste occasionally with the juices or more butter.

WHAT LIES AHEAD

I've been thinking a lot about how love looks,
about how I never saw my parents hold
each other's hands, about how I'd come in
from school and see my mother striding
across the kitchen floor singing "Que Será, Será"
while my father sat in his chair listening
to the *news*, writing a sermon, talking
on the phone, about never seeing them touch like
two lovers in heat at a dinner party or a rally
or after Bible study who couldn't wait
to get home (or at least the backseat
of the four-door, black-and-red Plymouth
she bought because his credit was burnt), about
how he'd say *No!* (*Come on, Al, let's go for a walk*) or
just ignore her (*Have you seen the keys? Al, I asked you
a question . . .*) about how she danced around the house
day after day like Nat King Cole was serenading her,
about the way she praised him after church,
then kissed him, with her eyes open,
on the cheek and rubbed her lipstick off,

about the only prurience that seemed to live
within their union: the fervent way she'd inch
closer to the edge of the green sofa and challenge
him during one of their impassioned disagreements
about racism or a family member who wronged him,
then she'd call his name, *But Al*, and eventually
there'd be silence, until the next morning's whispers
and laughter coming from their bedroom
that woke me up happy they'd made up, and wondering
if maybe they'd just had sex,
about how even though she left him after too many times
of being called *stupid* they stayed married for nearly fifty
     years,
about all the things I thought I knew about the way they
     loved,
about the way, when *your* mother and I are having
a conversation about living apart, and *your* eyes
fix on me like you're wondering why you never saw us
holding hands . . . why we never woke you up
at the break of dawn . . . how is it possible for two people
to just stop being together . . . I know that you're grading
me, too, and that this is a test I've probably failed
just like I thought they had.

I REMEMBER

One-hundred-degree summers
Riding backseat in Dad's nut-brown Ford Pinto,
after church, sweat clinging like static, our heads
out the window trying to catch a breeze
on our way to High's Ice Cream store—paradise

Fourth of July barbecues with cousins
unseen since last summer
bid whist and spades
dominoes slammed on tables
aunts cursing, uncles drinking, everyone
laughing, a family chorus
saying grace—grateful

The way Granny chased her chickens
the way she chased us with her switch
The stuff I found in Granddaddy's closet
an old Timex pocket watch
a bookmarked Bible
a pouch of silver dollars—Good times

The time we sat, steel-like in fear,
for two hours in the parking lot
of an Orlando hotel, Disney World a magnet,
because your grandfather couldn't find his hat—
    Bad times

The names I called my sister: Evil
the looks they shot me: Wicked
The way all was forgotten
when we finally climbed Space Mountain
The joy we found in traveling
and though we disliked packing,
how we didn't mind moving
New York. North Carolina. Virginia
all in the same year
in the same car
travel games
logging license plates in notebooks
falling asleep, the four of us stacked,
like firewood for winter—cramped

New school years
fresh clothes
winning the spelling bee
My father smiling
Making the honor roll
One dollar per A from my neighbor, Mrs. Patton
Relatives I've never met congratulating me—Proud

Loved ones who have passed
Uncle Richard. Granddaddy. Ovie. Granny.
Aunt Dorothy. Sergille. Granddaddy again. Nana.
Mommy.
Funerals, missing old folks, meeting new ones

Family meetings
which were more like lectures
with no Q&A
Trials with no jury — Guilty

The excitement around seven candles
and seven days in December
My mother's meat loaf
My father's macaroni and cheese
and mustard

Grocery store checkout line quizzes
If I have a coupon for fifty cents off
and today is double coupon day
and the Tropicana is two for three dollars
then what is the cost including tax?
No rewards for the right answer
consequences for the wrong

Monopoly with my siblings
laughing, crying, dreaming, planning,
loving and leaping forward into our futures

sitting in the living room
fingering through the countless memorabilia
that my mother kept
scrapbooks. yearbooks. old report cards. love letters.
    wedding photos.

I remember
looking for me
in all those moments
and finding love.

PART TWO

LIKE MIDNIGHT ENTERING SUNRISE

In one kiss, you'll know all I haven't said.

—Pablo Neruda

NOTE ON PILLOW

the heart is a small
but sacred place you are my
country your breasts, the

soft mountains I climb,
your lithe hips, the river that
swerves and curves in two

your candied tongue, the
morning fruit that bends inside
my lonely mouth.

What I mean to say
is that my pulse is all wild/
derness without the

whole of your body
beside me, without our naked
nightly rhapsody.

PORTRAIT OF A NEW LOVER: GENESIS

five minutes after
she reads his note

her smile explodes.
She wonders if he is the one

then decides to
Go into the washroom

where he is
you can call me

if you want," she says, laughing
like a river, or volcano.

she is Mars to him
and he wants to explore

every red canyon
every butterscotch moon

but he is unsure:
the geography of her

is both blessing
and curse

how do you not love
when the mere parting of lips

can swallow you whole
take your breath?

THIS IS HOW HE ASKS HER OUT

Give me your laugh
Give me the sound
of a million clouds
bursting
with a thunderous joy
and I will never close my eyes
when you are near me.

He says things
like this to her
all the time
on the phone.
A part of her wants him
to put it down
on paper   or text
so she can unravel
each muscular word.
The other part
just wants to laugh
out loud.

You can't say things
like that to me
while I'm working.
How is your book coming?

Ahhh yes, the book . . .
I am stuck on the part
where the woman
finally eats
after four and a half days
of mourning her lover
and I cannot decide whether
her first meal is breakfast
or salad. Or both.
What do you think?

Maybe she is thirsty,
so she pulls the cork
the wet legs on her glass
pressing for a sweet taste — then drinks
him in. That is what I think, she whispers
into the phone,

And since there are
no coworkers pacing behind him
no cubicles detaining him,
he laughs out loud.

I gotta run, she says.
Okay, but are we on? Will you let me
dive into your smile
swim from one corner of your mouth
to the other
carry it in my smile
like a wave
on the rising sea?

GOLDEN SHOVEL

After Paul Laurence Dunbar

It was two thousand eighteen when we
last saw each other. You were wear/
ing a mint-green, square-neck dress. The
ballroom, packed. This was before a mask
was *de rigueur*. I was speaking at that
Loews Hotel near Vanderbilt, inspiring grins
and tears from the teachers with my poems and
stories about love and death and *Nikki* and what lies
beneath the soil of human greatness? It
is between the pages of a book where possibility hides,
I remember you saying after dinner, right before our
first hug and then me kissing you on both cheeks
like we do in London. It'd been five years and
a lockdown when we met for lunch, you unmasked,
me fresh out of my hazmat suit from the flight, our
lips testing positive, a pandemic spreading in our eyes.

GEORGIA ON MY MIND

The first time we made love
we were in the Doubletree hotel
the one near the airport
in a room with two beds.
I remember going back and forth
in my mind
about which one to use
and then closing the curtains
because I didn't want you to see
I hadn't renewed my gym membership.

I found my way to your lips
in the near dark
and let my tongue travel
so far into the tunnel of your mouth
that I could taste your heart.
I remember it was just sweet enough
like the bottle of peach tea I knocked over
trying to silence my phone
and redirect my tongue
at the same time.

Freeing you
from your impervious sports bra
the bright brown nipples
poised for takeoff
landing inside you
like a plane on a runway
are all worthy memories
but the thing that poets never write about
the thing I remember the most
is how when it was over
and you put your gym clothes back on
and went to work out
I tossed the tea
did ninety-seven sit-ups
never opened the curtains
and heard the roar of a plane
wondering if it was leaving
or coming back.

APPETIZER

When we hugged
I am certain
I felt the moon
tugging the earth
each rise and fall
of your soft chest
melting into mine
a tinge of pumpkin curry
lingering between your lips
your partner
over by the bandstand
dancing in the dark
and suddenly I couldn't wait
for dinner
to be served.

HAIKU

Under quiet stars
we float   gravel grabbing our
feet   moon staring down

at our heads   both the
color of magnolia   my
placid hand inside

yours   each finger a
budding spring promise   the night
is beautiful   fire

flies flashing wings
beneath the cavalcade of
stars   branches of old

trees dance in the breeze
each an audience to our
secret rendezvous.

PORTRAIT OF A WOMAN: ACCRA, GHANA

Africa, I miss you
calling my name

holding the rhythm
of a forgotten history

in your seductive lilt
I see you woman

eyes ripe and round as coconut
hips like ocean

I watch you walk
the way of the palm

with each gentle sway, you bend me
I feel you, your ebullient breasts

like cresting billows, feed me
plantain and jollof

hope and happiness
I crave you Black star

like midnight
entering sunrise

like sunrise giving birth
to daybreak

my lips thirst
for your tomorrow

this is more than captivation
I am mere dragonfly

kissing your finger with my eyes open
longing to be held

like a swelling wave
beneath the copper sun

inside the golden abundance
that is your burning heart

JOLLOF CAESAR SALAD

Caesar salad is the perfect starter for dinner, and the perfect meal for lunch (or light dinner). And when you add the world-famous Ghanaian jollof spice to the mix, the party is about to *turn up*. It may seem like a pain to make—with all the pots and pans—but it's so worth it. It's healthy (I mean, at least we think it is, right?), and it's just plain good. I got the chicken version, the pescatarian version, whatever you desire. This creamy pan-African dish is the brand-new flavor for your tongue.

This, I'm making for a lover after we've both had a long day of work. It's hearty. It's tasty. And it's quick, so we can get to dessert sooner. What I'm listening to is "Love Tastes Like Strawberries" by Somi featuring Gregory Porter.

TOTAL TIME: 15 MINUTES

MAKES: 6-8 SERVINGS

CALORIES PER SERVING: 94

COURSE: SALAD/LIGHT DINNER

Ingredients

1 pound medium shrimp (or 2 boneless chicken
   breasts, cut into cubes)
2 tablespoons (or 1 if you can't take the heat) of jollof
   dry spice (1 teaspoon of each of the following
   mixed together: dried chili flakes, cinnamon,
   dried thyme, ground nutmeg, garlic powder,

ground ginger, ground coriander, allspice; and a
splidge of kosher salt, pepper, and Old Bay
seasoning if you're using shrimp).

1 tablespoon olive oil

1 head of fresh, crisp romaine lettuce chopped into
medium-size pieces

¼ cup grated Parmesan cheese

Your favorite Caesar dressing

1 tin of anchovy fillets, drained

Salt and pepper to taste

Optional: (tomatoes, avocado, croutons, 1 tablespoon
palm oil)

Instructions

Season the shrimp or chicken with the jollof spice mix.
Heat the oil in a frying pan on medium. Add the shrimp
or chicken to the pan and cook for 3 to 5 minutes or until
the folks upstairs start coughing from the spice in the air.
Set aside.

Put the chopped lettuce into a large bowl. Add the
Parmesan (and tomatoes and avocado should you desire
those), then add half the dressing and toss lightly. Top
with the shrimp or chicken, anchovies, and croutons,
then drizzle with the remaining dressing. Season with salt
and pepper. For that fancy Ghana flavor, sprinkle a little
palm oil over the salad.

HAIKU

Like a blackbird on
a raincloud—head raised, tail dipped
u rode me until

lightning struck us down.
Remember how i floated
away in your arms

after thunder came?
This is not a poem, just
a pining poet

quietly singing,
a fluted warble craving
u from storm to ground.

KUPENDA

I could say that
your lips
are soft clouds
of rain
that dance
on the horizon
at sunset
and my tongue catches
each sweet drop
of you, holds it
like a promise
or
that your embrace
is a cool breeze
in summer,
and the warm touch
of your calm fingers
on my head
makes me wanna holler
like a Baptist choir

singing Hallelujah
to the heavens
but
this is not
one of those long, loud poems
that goes
on and on, like
a roaring sea
or a midnight train
going west.

This is just me
remembering
the quiet way
you let me
tour your coast
from north
to south
the way
I floated up
and away
after kissing
you.

78

THREE WORDS

I no longer just want to be impressed.
I want the words
to hold water   to not sound
like an elegant answer
you've honed
for a job interview
or a throwaway line in a play
you're rehearsing.
Let them surprise me
with the glint of artless beauty
black pearls   rolling off your tongue
let them move me
like a strong rapid   so I may hold on
to the substantial air
of one simple, solemn oath.
Still me
like the first cry
of a newborn
like I mean the world
to you.

GOOD NIGHT

According to Google
there are five phases of sleep.
Somewhere between two
and three I shift to my right side
If you are woken up during this stage,
you may feel groggy and disoriented.
I move my hand from
my forehead, ready for the slow
delta waves of deep sleep
If phase three is too short, sleep
will not feel satisfying.
Are you awake, she asks?
I am on the edge of falling
Is someone calling my name?
Should I answer?
My wife is aware
that I am a light sleeper
she knows that the hint
of a glimmer or mild cacophony
will send me back to phase one:
The eyes are closed, but if aroused . . .
Wait,

Someone is calling my name
Are you awake?
I see her now. Leaning
against the cherry headboard. Staring
at me. Concerned, confounded,
curious. I wonder, have I forgotten
something significant. Birthday, anniversary,
dishes.
Why don't you write me
Love poems anymore?
She asks. At 3 a.m.
Should I answer?
I open the other eye
seeing her full-on
I sit up, inch a little
closer to her naked land
You are still my ocean,
My dear. Your hips my
soft raft. Those two lips the oars
I steer. You are the poem
If you were a couplet
I'd rhyme you
Okay, she smiles
Just don't haiku me
Take yr time
I want an epic
Anything else, my dear?
Well, since you're up
Can you take care of the dishes?

IF YOU WERE A COUPLET, I'D RHYME YOU

If you were a ladder
I'd climb you

Way up to the top
and I'd find you

If you were a doorway
I'd enter you

If you were unhinged
I'd center you

If you were a secret
I'd uncover you

Then seek out your treasure
rediscover you

If you were in front
I'd be behind you

Pull out some espresso
and grind you

Let's say you're a bossa
I'd hum you

Play you my guitar
and then strum you

If you weren't my wife
I'd wed you

then pull out a quilt
and I'd bed you

But, since you're my woman
I'll just love you

and kiss that sweet halo
above you.

PICTURING YOU

I am not a painter
browns and blues
we get along
but we
are not close
I am no
van Gogh
but give me
plain paper
a dull pencil
some Scotch
and I will
hijack your curves
take your soul
hostage
paint a portrait
so colorful and delicate
you just may have to
cut off my ear

A POET WALKS INTO A BOOKSTORE

she tells me they
only sell books about
social justice and
peace and that mine are mostly
about love and
relationships which they
don't promote.
i ask her if she thinks
changing the world by
herself is such a good
idea and how can you ever
be free without
someone to hold
i wonder how many
revolutions started with a
kiss how many communists Neruda
made love to how free it must
feel to walk through life
at peace
alone.

AN AMERICAN LOVE POEM

I want those championing freedom
the patriots of peace
the ones who march into our schools
handcuff our history
hold our imaginations hostage
the so-called American dreamers

I want them
to uncage their hearts
to cast off their chains of fear
to remember the bedtime stories
that comforted them
when nightmares chased sleep away

to remember the first-grade teachers
who read them pictured fables
that showed them how to love each other
and planted the seeds of possibility
that blossomed into their becoming

to remember how hopeful it felt
to be held by their mother's songs and poems
on nights when thunder
ravaged the sky.

I want them to know
that banning a book
is like banning a hug
and *that* is a dismal storm
no child should be left behind in.

PORTRAIT OF A WRITER

Lately
on the phone
when you get all fired up
over changing the world
and the new play you're writing about
the politics of undressing a womanist
(and why some men don't drink red wine)
I've become thirsty
and anxious
wondering
what it must have been like
for Harriet Tubman's lover
to come
with her.

LUNCH IN SAN FRANCISCO: 2017

Once after giving a speech about
how I didn't get cool until
I started making love with
words, then strutting off/
stage to a standing ovation, three
friends took me to the Mission District for flautas
and tepache and one of them—wearing
rimless glasses and an elegant smile that
curved perfectly around the best behaving
set of teeth I've ever seen—said
she didn't know what all the fuss was
about, that anyone could make librarians
swoon if they stood onstage for
an hour reading haiku about climbing
mountains and raising flags and slowly coming
down, that she wished she could write
lines that got women wet so they'd
buy her books like they do mine. I noticed
a stipple of crema lingering on her
mouth so I gently took my napkin, tapped her

bottom lip and asked her if she'd ever seen
Lucille Clifton's *magic hips* and then I may have
quoted something about a rod that twists
and is a serpent and she didn't blush, but no one said
anything else that mattered or that I remember but
when I saw her a year later holding a thick, black
ballpoint, autographing at some conference, I bought
a copy of her latest book of feminist free verse on
love and self-reflection and she thanked me and I
headed to the ballroom to give my speech about
how we sometimes find poems in the strangest
and most uncomfortable places.

AN UNLIKELY LOVE STORY

Let the beauty of what you love be what you do.

—Rumi

I didn't always want to be a writer. In fact, when I went to college, I wanted to get as far away from language and literature as possible. You see, your bookish grandparents—my father, a writer, professor, book publisher, and Baptist preacher; my mother, homemaker, storyteller, school principal, who also taught English at the local college—believed that books were reward. And punishment. We couldn't really watch television; it was always *Read a book*. With your grandmother, books were adventures, playdates, fun. But your grandfather treated words like millstones, not only ordering me to read Chinua Achebe, the encyclopedia, his dissertation, but assigning written reports and oral quizzes to the point where every ounce of reading joy was ground right out of me. Simply, I loathed books, so when Virginia Tech asked me to choose a major, I opted for biochemistry/premed. The most writing I would encounter in that profession would be prescriptions, and I could live with that. Then something happened. Actually, two somethings.

I met a remarkable woman on campus. She was tall, fashionable, with gleaming skin the color of nightfall. And lips that only poets wrote about. I was smitten, but with no game to actually let her know this, let alone woo her. So I picked up a book of love poems—Pablo Neruda or Sonia Sanchez—and became reacquainted with the joy and power of words on a page, of the right words in the right order. Then I wrote her love poems. And they worked, and we started dating. Later, we would get married near an old plantation on the James River and her mother would faint, either because it was oppressively hot, or because my father, the dashiki-wearing officiant, in some puzzling objection to the wedding tradition of enslaved Africans, had us jump *backward* over the broom (which confused everyone), or because she couldn't bear the thought of her only child, three months pregnant, getting married to a man who'd ditched the sciences to pursue a career as a poet. As Robert Graves wrote, *There is no poetry in money. But, then again, there is no money in poetry.*

The second thing that happened was Nikki Giovanni. The rock-star poet who published her first book the same year I was born: 1968. She's written dozens of bestselling books, won countless awards, been recognized by NASA and presidents. But you know she's the real deal if she's got a bat named after her. I knew she was the real deal, and in my second sophomore year, she became a visiting professor. I'd been loving her poetry since my mother read me her 1971 collection *Spin a Soft Black Song*. In fact, when my mother invited my sister and me to help name our newborn sister, just days after she returned home from the hospital, we unanimously decided on naming her after a character in that book, even though we had no idea what it meant. We just liked the rhythm of it, the uniqueness of it, the merry way it sounded on our tongues:

Come Nataki dance with me
Bring your pablum dance
with me
Pull your plait and whirl around
Come Nataki dance with me

There were pictures of Nikki, and books by Nikki, and stories about her art and activism all throughout my childhood and young adult life. How hard could her class be? I'd been reading poetry since I could walk. Her poetry, in fact. She's a legend. A fiery poet. On campus, I was a legend (in my own mind) and a fiery student leader. So when it was announced that she'd be teaching a poetry course, I signed up immediately. We wrote in each class, turned in our poems, and she graded them. Having imagined myself a good poet—with a girlfriend to prove it—I submitted several of my love poems. It should be noted that I cringe when I read some of these now, but alas, it's a part of the story, my story, so here goes:

Haiku
i knead you, feel you
shaping, rising, moist and warm
slowly coming round

My first grade in Nikki's class was a C-minus. I was disappointed, but not discouraged. I wrote more and better, I thought. At the end of the semester, when I received a final grade of C, I was a little disgruntled. But not defeated. When she announced she'd be teaching a class on Black studies the next school year, I signed up. Having grown up in a house with a father who'd forced me to read everything from Baraka to Du Bois, and having attended an independent Black elementary school in Brooklyn, New York, where Black studies was ninety percent of our learning, and having celebrated Kwanzaa my entire childhood, surely an Introduction to Black Studies course would be a cakewalk. It wasn't, and this time when I got the C, on our final exam—a poem about some social injustice I cared deeply about, maybe apartheid—I was baffled and angry. Noticing my displeasure, I guess, she asked me to stop by during office hours. It's about time she apologized for giving me a hard time, I thought to myself, for not acknowledging my genius with words.

I remember sitting down. I remember her telling me that *night comes softly.* And me saying, *Nikki, there's a storm coming.* Her telling me *Be bold…but be eloquent.* Me replying, *I am. Like Nancy Wilson singing "Save Your Love for Me."* I remember her taking a drag of her cigarette, blowing the smoke in my direction, then saying, *Kwame, go listen to Billie Holiday or Aretha. You are a good poet, and I can teach you the tools, but I can't teach you to be interesting.* I stood up, stormed out of her office, and decided that sometimes your heroes and idols are not good people. I didn't speak to her for an entire semester.

A year went by before I calmed down enough to enroll in

yet another class with Nikki Giovanni. The course was Children's Literature 101. I had no interest in writing children's literature, but I'd convinced myself that it was probably an easy course, and as I was a senior with the singular focus of spending my final semester with as few challenging classes as possible, it made sense. When I look back on this decision, I suppose I was a glutton for punishment. There was no way this was going to end well. And it didn't. She'd assigned us to write a poem in the voice of and from the perspective of a child. I wrote and performed a poem — "Daddy" — about your grandfather and how much he traveled and how I occasionally missed him:

Wednesday nights don't make me feel
too good

I toss and turn
in my bed thinking
of Thursday morning
the day i gotta get up extra early
to hear Momma scream
"Take out the trash, boy"

So i get up
and put on whatever
is lying on the floor
next to me
that i was supposed to put in the hamper
yesterday.
Then i put on my hat

Walking through the house is always fun
i can stop by the kitchen and steal
some of the cake that
Momma told us not to touch
It's a good kind of feeling to be the only one up
get some milk, and watch all the ladies
on TV try and lose weight.
Then i get some orange juice.

Standing in the doorway
i see Momma with her belt
in my mind
and quickly remember that
i'm supposed to take out all the trash
in the house
and anything else i see lying around.

So then i finally get all the bags together
and take out the trash.
The more trash i find
the cleaner the house is
and the nicer she will be to us
and then i think of Daddy.

She gave me a C.
I remember that one of the red-inked notes in my margins
was *Why the lowercase "i"?* I wanted to say *Because you make
me feel so small.* This was the last thread of hope that Nikki

Giovanni and I would be anything more than adversaries. She didn't like me, and I didn't like her.

That semester, I used my words to deal with my frustration and anger. I wrote a play, and in that play there just *happened* to be a character who was a wicked college professor who smoked incessantly. It was a tragicomedy about all the things wrong with the professor's way of teaching, and with her. I cast it. I directed it. And I staged it on the campus of Virginia Tech. The audience was packed and silent, in shock. No matter, I got the final word, and my ego was restored. It got back to Nikki that I'd written an unfavorable play about her, which I didn't admit to. Nor did I challenge her directly. Because she didn't like me, and I didn't like her.

Five years later, I was newly divorced—seems my mother-in-law was right about poetry not being a sustainable career for a twentysomething husband and father to a four-year-old—and the author of a book of amateurish, if not provocative, love poems that I published myself. Having a father who taught me the ins and outs of book publishing proved beneficial. I promoted my debut collection by performing poems and selling books at open mics, at churches, at subway stops, and at any event that allowed exhibitors and vendors to sell their wares. One such event was the three-day inaugural Furious Flower Poetry Conference held at James Madison University.

I'd purchased an exhibitor table for $100 and over the course of the conference convinced, enticed, begged attendees to buy a copy of my book. On the last day, I was basking in the light of success, having sold most of my stock, when a woman came up to me and asked to buy two copies. I did a double take because this couldn't be happening. It was Nikki Giovanni. She gave me a $20 bill, said thank you, took her books, and walked away. This had to be a prank, or a dream, because she didn't like me, and I didn't like her.

Over the next few years, I'd see her at one literary event or another—the National Black Arts Festival in Atlanta, Carroll Hardy's Student Leadership Conference at the College of William & Mary, Toni Morrison's sixtieth-birthday party in Philly—and each time I'd try my best to avoid her. Once, we found ourselves at the same place, in the same room, at the same time, and chatting seemed ineludible. It was here that she congratulated me on the books—by then, I'd also edited and self-published a book about the life and death of Tupac Shakur— then asked if I wanted to contribute a poem to an anthology on grandfathers she was editing for Henry Holt and Company. I nodded, gave her my address to send the information, and walked away weary of the interaction, because we didn't really like each other. So why was she offering up this opportunity?

Behind your house
Nandi and I will go walking
across the earth's cold floor
past the chicken coop that is no longer there
and I'll stop suddenly and tell her "Shhh"
and she'll ask "What are you listenin' for?"
and I'll say "Listenin' to—dinner"
and with your big eyes she'll look at me
strange for a cold minute

until I tell her the stories
of how you broke bread
with those chickens, fattening them
until Granny cracked their necks
and fried their legs
and again she'll say "Ugh"
and then I'll show her the new Masonic Lodge
which used to be the old Masonic Lodge
which used to be the meeting place
for those angry negro folks
preaching about taking us back to Africa.
and she'll ask, "Did he go with them?"
and I'll smile and rub her head
the way your son used to rub mine
when I made him smile.

And then, when we arrive at your gravesite...

It was the longest poem I'd ever written. An ode to Albert Tilton Alexander. Five hundred and sixty-seven words. Three pages. It took me a month to get it just right, to feel comfortable enough to submit it. And when I did, it was like Virginia Tech all over again. No response. No indication whether she'd accepted it or not. It was just me, left with my own insecure writerly thoughts that the poem just didn't cut it. It misbehaved, as Nikki would often say in class. The whole thing had been a setup. I was about to get another C. And then something happened.

Dear Kwame, the letter read, *I am happy to accept your*

poem, The Remembering. Your grandfather would be proud. And so am I. It is not a lot, but please find the enclosed check for fifty dollars as payment. Love, Nikki!

By the time her anthology was published, I'd written a few more books, mailed them to her, and she'd written nice thank-you notes. We even exchanged a few letters that had nothing to do with poetry. We talked about mothers and meat loaf and made promises to have dinner together soon. In none of these letters did we ever talk about our time together at Virginia Tech. I surmised that Nikki probably didn't dislike me anymore. So I stopped disliking her. When I published my seventh collection of love poems, I was visiting St. Louis to appear at a poetry celebration at a local jazz club. The morning of, I open my hotel door to get my room-service breakfast and the server hands me a newspaper. As I'm eating my pancakes, I turn to the arts section and staring at me is a big old picture of me. The brief article details my evening performance and there are also a few quotes about my poetry, from the event organizer and some local poets, but the quote that knocks me off my feet is this:

If I can have a literary son, I like to think it is Kwame Alexander. Hard worker; truth seeker; soul sharer.—Nikki Giovanni

It was around this time that I started feeling guilty about the awful things that I'd thought, and said, and written about her in college. I confessed my remorse to mutual friends, who assured me that she'd forgiven me. I wrote her letters fawning over her new poems, even called her several times just to gab and gossip. I wrote poems about her:

If you were a song
I'd call you jazz

Clap for you
Snap to you

Sing with you
Swing with you

I'd color you Ellington
Elegant and Essential in my life

In interviews about my burgeoning writing career—I was now writing children's literature—when asked who my greatest inspirations were, I'd talk about how my parents introduced me to the power of words, and it was Nikki Giovanni who showed me how to make them dance on the page. We appeared on stages together—reading poetry, interviewing each other, paying tribute to legends like Lucille Clifton and Maya Angelou, laughing. We loved our time together so much that we began traveling together. It was on one of our visits to Ghana, in West Africa (we went twice), to train teachers and build a library, that we visited Kakum National Park's rain forest, and she tried to convince me to walk across three canopies, and when I declined, she pushed me ahead of her onto the man-made walkway 130 feet above the ground. It'd been nearly twenty-five years, and in all our communications and adventures, neither one of us had ever mentioned what had happened at Virginia Tech. Until her mother died.

She called and said I needed to drive to her house so that we could drink beer. You see, her mother was a devoted beer drinker, and Nikki wanted to celebrate her passing by drinking the most expensive beer in the world—Samuel Adams Utopias. It costs upwards of $250 for a bottle. Because only an extremely limited amount is brewed each year, she was having difficulty securing a bottle. But she appeared on National Public Radio, sharing how she knew her mommy was dying when she said she didn't want a beer because every day of her life, she drank a beer. And then Nikki started to complain that she couldn't find Utopias, and the guy who makes Utopias heard it. And he actually sent it to her. A case of six. And she called me and said, "Kwame, I got the stuff."

We sat at her dinner table and broke bread. Grilled tuna and au gratin potatoes. And I remember it was my first time eating Brussels sprouts, and I ate two bowls, and we gossiped, and she told stories, and we drank wine, and then after dessert she brought out the Utopias. It was in a custom ceramic bottle, and it tasted so good. Not like beer. With just the perfect hint of black cherry. We consumed nearly two and a half bottles, a liter and a half, and we were quite happy way past midnight when it hit me. The decades-long guilt was too much for this poet's soul. I broke out crying, uncontrollably. Then she started crying, in the way that crying can be contagious. We were a sight, the two of us, tipsy, in tears. "I'm sorry, Nikki," I blurted out, "for all the mean things I said, for being pissed that you gave me Cs, for everything I did back in college." She looked at me, and the crying turned into laughter. The kind of laughter that comes out when you know something the other person doesn't. She shook her head, smiled, and said, *What are you talking about, I didn't give you a C. My goal as your teacher was to help you become the best you. I'm sure I saw your talent and I think if I actually gave you a C, it was to help you see your talent too. Knowing you, it probably upset you and made you work harder. Didn't it?*

When my mommy passed away years later, I called Nikki and told her. She asked for the funeral details, and I told her I would call her back with them. I never did, because I didn't want her to feel obligated to come to the funeral. You see, Nikki, like me, doesn't like going to funerals. Something about wanting to remember people as you last engaged with them, as you last chatted, as you last shared a meal, as you last laughed, as you last saw them. The night before the funeral, it was a Thursday, she called. *Kwame, I'm here in the hotel. I've written something for Barbara I'd like to share tomorrow at the funeral.* Without thinking, or thanking her, I said, *Nikki, you didn't have to come.* Nikki Giovanni has never cursed at me but one time, and this was it: *Kwame, why in the [insert swearword] would I not be there? You need to know you're not alone, that you still have a mother who loves you.*

> . . . We burst with pride
> at the Best Sellers
> and the Prizes
> But mostly I think we
>   Appreciate
> the warmth
> of the arms of our sons

laying us to rest
 knowing
we have done
A Good Job.

Take from this what you will, my dears. The lesson I took is that there are going to be people in your lives who did not change your diapers, who did not plan your birthday parties, who did not spank you, who did not force you to read books, who did not worry every time you had a sleepover, or went to a school dance, who will show you something significant and meaningful that will matter in your life even when you think it doesn't. There will be people who will honestly love you like I do. Like your mother does. So when you find your Ms. Giovanni, don't do like I did. Open your arms immediately and welcome her. And don't write a play about her.

In 2004, Texas Tech professor of biological sciences Robert Baker named a bat species he discovered in Ecuador after Ms. Giovanni. You know, bats, unlike flying squirrels and gliding possums, are the only mammals naturally capable of true and sustained flight. Nikki's been writing books for more than fifty-four years, and she recently retired after thirty-five years of teaching. Talk about sustained flight, a combined almost-centennial of Nikki's feeling, of Nikki's talking, of Nikki's judgment. And we are all the better for it. If I could have a literary mother, I'd like to say it is Nikki Giovanni.

PORTRAIT OF A MAN LISTENING TO JAZZ

He falls asleep humming her
sweet soprano dancing between
the stars this nightwoman reaches
inside him   her music tattooed across
an impenetrable umbra he dreams her body
of music a moonlight serenade that lulls
his midnight blues her *a cappella* a big, wide
grin the lyrics like schoolchildren chasing
Friday like church folk eating Sunday
this is how he wants to live looking
to the sky the days wandering away like clouds
inside her soft, strong sound cradled in the bosom
of hope   last night he fell asleep chanting her
song and woke up entranced in a fervid
sea of wonder with the sun on his tongue

PORTRAIT OF A MARRIAGE

I.
Those of us who know
passion know that lovers of
sun begin in heat

when the sizzle is easy
that to be inside a heart
beating is a drum

catching fire
an unquenchable thirst
every breath a wave

each kiss an incantation
an insatiable flame that flutters
like an autumn butterfly.

II.
Those who bathe in the
seriousness of marriage
know the river turns

that it carries storm
holds lightning in its hand
and like a concert of wolves

drowning their blues
sometimes the still of water
comes from the echo

of a soft song
of a single melody repeated
like ripples on a pond

Remember, love is as simple
as the opening
of a window

A steady hand
A devoted smile
A clean kitchen

Forging a union
of two is work
daily compromise
nightly labor—the heavy lifting
of precious ego

These are the things that matter
the linchpin architecture
that builds each season
brick by brick
that keeps us unbound
and nearly engulfed
carefully constructing
tomorrow.

TRANSITIONS

In the beginning
when life is lush
when you're hitting all the notes
following all the right chords
listening to each other
finding freedom
in each breath of devotion
every word coming softly
even the blues
got you wrapped up
in the magic
of some crazy love.

The music is so good.

Then something happens
maybe one of you screws up the changes
or the other forgets the lyrics to the next verse
and suddenly the whole sky is falling
into a turbulent sea

your world, filled with sullen gray faces
I want you to
keep playing
keep singing
keep loving
I want you to listen
to Ella in Berlin
invent a new sound,
a new star.

I want you to remember
that mistakes are opportunities
to know that if you can make it
to the end of the song
you've got something real
something to build
a world with.

PART THREE

INSTRUCTIONS FOR LEAVING

You will lose someone you can't live without,
and your heart will be badly broken, and the bad news
is that you never completely get over the loss
of your beloved. But this is also the good news.
They live forever in your broken heart
that doesn't seal back up. And you come through.

—Anne Lamott

Dear Samayah,

The last meal I shared with your grandmother was in a capacious hospital room in Chesapeake, Virginia. It was breakfast time, and the sun was a carefree soul galloping through the window like a wild horse. Having not eaten much in the forty-eight hours since she'd been admitted with complications of sarcoidosis, she was quite hungry. So I fed her. Spooned the applesauce. Placed in her mouth a few ice chips from the water glass she couldn't finish (crunching ice always gratified her). That was 2017. The year my heart broke into a million jagged puzzle pieces.

None of us is ever prepared for death. When a great tree falls, the birds, with no branch to perch on, scatter. Looking for a new home. In the nearly six years since my graceful mother has passed, I've been searching. Thumbing through old scrapbooks, sprinkling her ashes in places we lived and traveled—Brooklyn and St. Croix and Fayetteville, North Carolina—all in an effort to find some solace. To find a new home.

In 2018, when the American School in London invited me to become its inaugural Innovator-in-Residence, I welcomed the opportunity for that solace, along with a professional reboot. I'd gotten into a writing rhythm that, while successful, felt almost too comfortable. The process of coming up with a beginning, middle, and end was akin to riding a bike for me, and I could cruise through a story, arms akimbo, head to the wind. I needed to challenge my storytelling normal, become inspired in new and exciting ways, learn to pop a wheelie.

Part of moving yourself forward in a life-giving way is to take the things from the past that have helped shape and mold you and use them as anchors to the future. My own vision of what lay ahead came during two farewell dinners hosted by friends in the summer of 2019. First, award-winning children's book writer and illustrator Melissa Sweet crafted homemade lobster rolls the size of my arms in her palsy-walsy Maine home. Then I drove south to dine alfresco—grilled snapper, cheddar biscuits, Summer in a Bottle rosé—in celebration of Jacqueline Woodson's latest novel at her family's country estate. These two women not only burned in the kitchen but laughed and told stories and answered phone calls and helped with homework and listened. At the same time. With the cool and calm of a river flowing in a forest. Just like my mother used to do. Determined to do the same, the new Kwame would find his way home not only by moving to London but by cooking.

In my first few weeks there, I figured out how to catch a bus to Maida Vale, write at an outdoor café while sipping English Breakfast tea, and take refuge at the bottom of the London Library when it rained. I also learned to make some pretty tasty pasta—fettuccine Alfredo, spinach lasagna.

As the weeks turned to months, I discovered the best walking route to your new school. I learned how to listen and acknowledge your cries for independence and smile when you grabbed my hand and held it, our fingers braided like the cornrows your mother designed. I learned how to answer your not-so-random questions: *Why can't we get a car? Why do you have to walk me the whole way? Can we have a break from pasta . . . and make Granny's fried chicken for dinner?*

"If you read good books, when you write, good books will come out of you," wrote Natalie Goldberg in *Writing Down the Bones.* Thus, I imagined, if I read good cookbooks, good food would come out of my kitchen. So I immersed myself in a plethora of cooking primers, instructional videos, and blogs. I cooked daily while listening to music, helping you with homework, and just being in the moment. My recipe file fattened. Some meals turned out delicious the first time: fish chowder. Ghanaian red red. Lobster mac and cheese (which almost didn't happen 'cause lobster meat in London is more expensive than beluga caviar). Others required experimentation: Tuscan bread salad. Blueberry scones. Beer-battered fish. Unfortunately, my buttermilk pancakes looked, and tasted, more like crepes. Fortunately, you love crepes. But you also love chicken, and you kept asking me to make it.

During my adolescent summers, my mother often took us to Virginia Beach, where we'd spend the day building sandcastles, swimming too far out, and screaming bloody murder when we got stung by a jellyfish. Two things loom large in those memories. One was this: as hungry as we were from playing in the water, we hated getting out of it for lunch because of my mother's belief that one must wait thirty minutes to swim after eating (or face severe cramps due to lack of blood flow to the stomach and thus drown). The other: once we bit into one of my mother's crispy, juicy fried chicken drumsticks, the complaining stopped. She charmed us.

Until the age of five, you were a vegetarian—until we sent you to my mother's for a weekend summer vacation. As the story goes, Granny packed the three visiting grandchildren into her burgundy Hyundai one Saturday morning and carted them off to Virginia Beach for a day of swimming and sandcastles. Around midday she summoned each of you from the water and handed out brown paper bags full of chicken. When you came home, I understood the resoluteness in your smile when you claimed, "Daddy, I'm not a vegetarian anymore."

Fried chicken was one of my mother's signature dishes, as it was my grandmother's, and her grandmother's before that. Now that I wanted to continue the tradition for my family in my modest London kitchen, I needed the recipe. So I called around to my sisters, my aunts, even my father (who only ever lovingly made two dishes, mustard mac and cheese and tad-too-bland baked chicken). But I got the same answer from each of them: *There is no recipe.* They simply used a little bit of this and a little bit of that and cooked it until it was done. These reveals were often followed by joyous remembrances of picnics and Sunday dinners and family reunions, and every now and then I'd get a clue: *Barbara had that cast-iron skillet. Your grandmother used Crisco. The paper bag? They say it's to better coat the chicken, but we only used it 'cause Momma used it. Garlic powder. Paprika. And don't forget the oil has gotta be hot!*

This is how I began putting the pieces of my puzzle back together again. I'd go to the butcher down the block and buy six wings and two breasts one day, four thighs and five legs another. Try to remember my mother in the kitchen — her fingers covered in flour, her jubilant singing filling the room, her seasoned spirit. Imagine and reimagine the ingredients in her brown paper bag. See her placing the chicken in her pan, allowing each piece room to breathe. And every time I cooked, I felt a little bit closer to her, perched on a branch of her life.

Frying chicken right can feel like riding a bike backward. Or writing a sonnet. It's hard, sometimes elusive. But there is a form to guide you, and with practice you can find the flow. For me it took a dozen tries, and yet the ecstatic look on your face when you bit into that twelfth and final chicken wing was worth the wait. You got what you'd asked for. So did I. Through cooking I'd reunited with my mother, forged a powerful kinship. It was life-giving.

This one beautiful life is a series of puzzles. If you're fortunate, you get someone to show you how they fit together. If you're really lucky, when they're gone, you learn how to let their memory guide you, gather you, love you. So that when you get sad and unsure—because this new puzzle seems undoable—at least you have the precious memories to feed you while you put the pieces back together and find your way home.

BARBARA'S PICNIC FRIED CHICKEN

It took poet me twelve tries to re-create my mother's perfectly crispy-juicy fried chicken. There just isn't anything more delicious than a crunchy piece of finger-licking-good fried chicken. It might seem daunting, and it does require some trial and error, some focus and experimentation, but as long as you have some patience (and a brown paper bag), you're on your way to the absolute best fried chicken ever. Trust me on this.

I'm making this for Samayah only. Five pieces or twenty. She's going to eat them all. What I'm listening to is the *Nancy Wilson/Cannonball Adderley* album. (By the time you get to "One Man's Dream," you should be done!)

TOTAL TIME: 40 MINUTES

MAKES: 4 SERVINGS

CALORIES PER SERVING (3 PIECES): 840

COURSE: LUNCH OR DINNER

Ingredients

A 3-pound chicken, washed and dried and cut into
10 pieces (2 wings, 4 half breasts, 2 thighs, and
2 drumsticks—Note: sometimes I substitute a
big bag of wings)

5 teaspoons Diamond Crystal salt or 2½ teaspoons
Morton coarse kosher salt

2½ teaspoons freshly ground black pepper

Poultry seasoning to taste, if desired

2 cups all-purpose flour

⅓ teaspoon mild curry powder

2 teaspoons paprika

¼ teaspoon smoked paprika

¼ teaspoon ground cumin

2¾ teaspoons garlic powder, divided

Vegetable oil for frying: 4 to 5 cups

Instructions

Arrange the cut-up chicken on a rimmed baking sheet; sprinkle all over with half of the paprika, garlic powder, and salt and pepper (and poultry seasoning if you're using it). Let sit at room temperature 15 minutes, or chill, uncovered, up to 6 hours.

In a medium paper bag, combine the flour, curry powder, paprika, smoked paprika, cumin, the remaining salt and pepper, and the garlic powder. Close the bag and shake well to combine. Add the chicken to the bag, close, and shake well to coat.

Pour the oil into a large cast-iron skillet or Dutch oven to come 1 inch up the sides. Working in two batches and returning the oil to 350 degrees between batches, cook the chicken pieces, turning halfway through, until deep golden brown, 10 to 15 minutes per batch. (You can get REAL fancy and insert an instant-read thermometer into each piece…should register 160 degrees for light meat and 165 degrees for dark.) Transfer the fried chicken to a wire rack and let cool slightly before serving.

DINNER WITH NIKKI

One day someone's gonna ask
me what was it like to sit
at your mahogany dining table drinking
two-hundred-dollar beer, listening
to Motown, and they're gonna want
to know who we gossiped about, what stories
your walls held, whether you cooked
as good as your poems, and I'll smile
remembering the first time I ate
Brussels sprouts, or tasted lamb—the rosemary and
garlic bathed on my fingertips, begging
for a kiss—how I wasn't too proud to beg
for seconds and how we poured
Utopian libations, bottle after bottle, celebrating
Mandela and Maya and Toni and Aretha and Rap
and Tupac, chasing memory, battling tears long
into the silent night, and how dessert—some
fancy, petite pie with a subtle sweetness—from
the bakery on Main Street would fatten
the conversation back up until a name popped

out or a new book we were both reading
came up and I'd talk about how I didn't
care for the author's choices and say *Nikki, what
did you think?* and you'd call it like you always
do, say the thing I was really thinking, that
It's shit, and I'd laugh, then you'd explain what
you meant, not in the way one would defend
oneself, but in a matter-of-fact, professorial kind of
way, like you used to do in Advanced Poetry Seminar,
and by this point I'd be the choir, and you'd be
the preacher, and together we'd remember
the same tales differently and Ginney would shake
her head at our selective storytelling then get up
to let Alex out into the garage because he was barking,
and she'd return with another bottle
and you'd remind me to say hello to my father,
or as you call him, *The General*, and a song would come
on, say, "How Sweet It Is to be Loved by You,"
and somewhere close to morning, we'd
both remember the two women who loved us
the most, and toast our mothers, try to
swallow each troubled breath, and then
when there was nothing more to say,
nothing left to drink,
you could almost taste the near-perfect poems
lingering on my tongue and yours.

MY FATHER'S EULOGY

My father
rests alone
at home
and questions why
his sisters
chose
another preacher
to pray.
The last time
his mother died
they did
the same
but he obliged
and sat beside
another preacher
who said goodbye
to Granny.
Only this time
he couldn't
bear the thought

of losing
twice.
And so
at home
alone
he sat away
from flowers
open graves
saving tears
for the future's
sure unrest
endless nights
spent reciting
his father's eulogy
to himself.

FAREWELL

to Berlyn Cedric Howard

What I never told you
is that I wanted to be like you
all the girls naming you
cute and sweetheart
the way you walked
comfortably and coolly
wooing the world
with your dazzling smile
and muscular laugh
your skin ripened as a Bosc pear
You were bronze bald before Michael
and each time you knocked on my door
I saw spring
in your scalp
and I couldn't wait for us
to wander and wonder
to go meet the sun
together.

What I never told you is
that you were my hero
and now that you are gone
a young root shaken free of soil
I busy myself seeking the bones
of a friendship
in poems
and letters to myself
wearing your memory
like a shiny cape
not wanting to say goodbye
to the body
to the soul
of our childhood
and gratefully remembering
the way I soared
because you did.

JACQUELINE WOODSON

This is what I know
friendship is an art
and this canvas called life
can be vast and lonesome
without a full heart to trust
without a joyful noise to share
without you

LOVE STORY

1.
on the bus ride   home
from his first concert
they argue like Africans
in traffic

he fumes at the way she melted
like sub-Saharan shea butter
when the old, bald guy from work
a painter   in his spare time   told her
she could borrow his used brown Saab
until they got back   on their feet
and then bragged about the time
he rode an elevator with Sade
that he was so close he could count the beats
of her pulse   then drove straight home
and sketched her   full body
from floor   to ceiling.

Later   in bed reading
Alice Walker   by night-light
his heart is muted   their backs
two gridlocked bumpers   parked
under quiet stars

He has almost said something   sixteen times
when she rubs his scalp takes the book
out of his hands   reads
to him   the way she sprinkles jazz
in his ear tempts his familiar
turns him   around

2.
the next evening after leftover ramen
curled up   on the couch   watching
the baseball game   volume down
she comments on how number thirteen
just grabbed the ball   ran
up the middle   and almost hit it
out of the park and he wants to laugh
so loud at the wonderful jumble
of metaphors   but instead   he leaps up
like he's catching   an alley-oop
then sprints   to put the dishes away
so they can play

3.

From the kitchen   he glimpses
her calf the left one   dangling
a smooth, satisfying curve   a trumpet
blowing his mind   He wants her

The last black pot glistens   Its lid
a sweet silver flash   He holds the fork
like a bedtime ritual   carefully bathes each tine
You see, the dishwasher is too loud
plus, he gets to listen to jazz   but
when he is almost finished   ready to round
the bases   he hears the troubled water   a cacophonic
    wave
of salt and sorrow   she is listening to the news
again something about a boy and Skittles
and rain and blood and the weight
of being Black

Before there is ocean he turns down
Autumn Leaves, hollers: *You know it's National Poetry*
    Month, right?
Maybe tonight I'll pen you   *a pantoum*   She
    doesn't laugh
at his sly prurience   like she used to   but she does
    flip
the channel   it lands on *Jeopardy!*
the category   math: *What is I want is more*   *I want*

the whole geometry of you   connect me with those lines
of leg and toe   elbow and neck

The last dish cleaned   he moves to her   lifts
carries   places   peels off
her shiny stockings   This is where I want to be, he thinks
But right before he can divide her   above
the unpredictable sound of Miles   he hears
the complexity of their love   he hears
the sweet thunder that is life   *I'm leaving*

4.

They met in college   at a church barbecue
he was reciting a poem about how
you should never mix citrus fruits with melons
she was praise dancing   carrying
a crab leg   like a torch

for a year, all they did was smile   each morning
at seven-thirty   in line for breakfast   but
this day was different *You're the poet*   came a voice
from behind his chair   he swallowed because
      spitting
watermelon seeds was not an option

May I sit down she asked   shaking
his sticky hand he welcomed her, of course
eyeing her   dancer legs those calves
will be the end of me, he thought

The next weekend   she invited him to see
Spandau Ballet and when he explained
that while he loved to dance he just wasn't into ballet
and would she mind if they just caught *Footloose*
at the Lyric she kissed him on the cheek
like his neighbor   Mrs. Cuffee had done
when he showed up to trim her hedges for seven dollars
then pulled out his mother's kitchen scissors

Before the movie   he made her dinner:
Rice-A-Roni   and baked chicken   But
it was the dessert the blueberry scones and the listening
to Marvin all night long that molded her heart
and shaped her love that made her legs rise
like two piccolo trumpets dancing naked
under the moon

They never made it to the Lyric   A week later
she moved in with her Bible   her retainers   her soft-
rock albums   and a sweet-smelling orange blossom
that she mixed with warm milk   and honey
for their baths   He was thunderstruck

5.
After he introduced her to Nancy Wilson   and
     Cannonball Adderley
she taught him the secret   to a good omelet: chili
powder   They overslept   regularly
skipping classes reading to each other planning a future

The way she woke him each day was epic
and electric

6.

And five years later   it is over just like that?
She holds his hand   to her chest   tells him
that she is still a word woman   that
first and foremost she will always love
the way he colors her   line by line
word by binding word   but   that
metaphors cannot pay the mortgage that
there are no stock options   for literary photographers
of passion and pain   that
dentists don't accept concise wordplay as payment
that all the beautiful music in the world don't mean a thing
if we don't have a vehicle   to carry   the hopes
and dreams   in our heart.

7.

The next day   when he watches her drive
away   in the two-door metallic gift   to the sound
of a runner   stealing home   in the ninth inning he
    knows
the masquerade is over   and so is love   and so
is love

WITHOUT U

i am lost
as in: isolated
unfinished broken off
shipwrecked on the shore of solitude
ankle-deep in possibility
i have read the dictionary   twice
and still there r no words
to fill my blank spaces
to punctuate the way i feel
when your smile dances
across the stucco walls
of my memory   perhaps
i will open a thesaurus now
and find a little piece of hope
or something similar

BENEFITS OF FIGHTING

The time I told you I'd kissed
my ex-girlfriend and I needed
some time, and you said
Okay and we kept walking
to *7-Eleven for a Slurpee* like you hadn't
just swallowed an earthquake

The time you didn't come
to bed until after I'd
gotten up to use the
bathroom for the second time
this was three months into
our marriage and you were
already replacing me with
late-night reruns of *Mad About You*
and I just closed my eyes
trying to evade the rising
sea by naming titles of
all the plays I was yet to write

The time I raised my voice
at our nervy six-year-old because
she hadn't made her bed
again or she lied about brushing
her teeth and I needed her to
know these things were
unacceptable and you told
me we would not be those
kind of parents who shouted
at their kids and to avoid
any drama we both just stopped
talking about it then later
we got a babysitter and went
to the movies and sat next to
each other laughing at Adam
Sandler, eating from our own
buckets of popcorn and I never
offered you a bite of my
oatmeal chocolate chip and we
didn't touch, not even a leg or elbow

The times we never fought
over things that meant nothing
and everything, that mattered
to who we were becoming

The times we never got to protect
our boundaries because we stayed
in bounds because it was easy because
the blues is hard as whiskey and
we stayed happily sober

The times we never got to drive
each other mad, our hearts
stalled engines questioning if
this was going anywhere but
never answering the truth
that we never got to fix
a thing because we pretended
they weren't broken

All the times we never got to
make up never got to make
love never got to make us
into something
real.

PORTRAIT OF A DIVORCE

You opened the door
on the fifth knock
the distance between us
a thousand miserable miles
and I remember feeling defeated
at not having a key
to my own wife's apartment.

When you asked me to cook for you
Greek pasta
a flame of home lit in me
and when I reminded you
that they'd probably stolen it
from the Egyptians (and just added feta cheese)
you laughed like you used to
when I'd write a funny love poem
or you saw a photograph
of Clarence Thomas drinking
a Pepsi.

After we ate
in silence
our three-year-old asleep
in the next room
you matter-of-factly lifted your black dress
just above your waist
and let me make love to you
right there on the hardwood
next to the dining table
I knew something was different
because you kept your eyes open the whole time
like you wanted to remember me

When we finished
and the door shut behind me
I felt split in two
a cracking of a pyramid
the severing of a family
and I knew
you'd never see me again
like that, and
I'd never be the same,
whole.

THOUGHT

Our love was anchored
in real vision
and friendship.
We waved at Venus
like she was a neighbor.

We fellowshipped
in the church of big ideas
longed for fertile ventures.
We planned our wedding
like a start-up.

Our mission never waned
So we got down to business
We stargazed castles
devoted ourselves to working
twelve-hour days

We built a world
We built You
in the moments
outside of work
between the dreams.

And when we got what we wanted
What we envisioned
What we worked overtime for
All these years
There was nothing left
of us
for us
to do
together

We thought we were lovers
turns out we were partners
constructing a meaningful livelihood
We were best friends
who love each other
and now we are two ships
we pass . . .
and speak to each other in passing . . .

A LETTER TO MY WIFE

i wanted to write you
a letter, a testimony,
one last awkward love poem
on the eve of our divorce
to tell you a few important things
about the union of
our hope
and our hearts
how this slow death
of what was us, little by little
year by year
is not the end of our story.

but where to start?
our honeymoon picture.

the way you stood
perfect and precious
like my very own Aphrodite
your breasts, like statues

my eyes liquid, all over you
me afraid to touch, wanting
to be respectful, patient even
and how every therapist
since has told me
how I failed you
in that moment,
that even though my memory
is pleasant and joyous, us
sitting on the beach
planning out our life, our
incessant laughter
at the way the waiter said Lime-ade,
that, indeed, this may have been
the beginning,
of our unraveling
before our marriage had barely begun.

before us
when i was nothing more
than clay, unformed.
a manchild
I often think of those
early years, unsure
and bewildered
my romantic confidence
as low as my credit score
and each night, too ashamed to hold you
and too cool to demand to be held.

although i had the will to change,
i didn't have the skill.
nor knowledge of how to learn
to love myself fully
so i could love you and us
fully.
i am sorry is not enough
is a water bottle trying to hold an ocean
of atonement.

i used to joke about how
you loved to practice your degree
in psychology on friends
never realizing
that i was patient zero,
and our marriage was
a master class
in tolerance and persistence
in how to lovingly mold a man
into someone significant,
someone who believed
in himself.

but how to finish?

i've wondered if i could go back
would i have given up what we found
for what we missed
and the answer scares me

because i love who i am
who you helped me become
and that kind of makes up
for all the reasons why
we no longer wake up
beside each other.

kind of.

That i have not been as tolerant
and persistent in my commitment
is my only regret.
no, in fact, this is one of many regrets, my dear,
many of which i've written about
in these pages.

there will be new lovers
who come into our lives
who will kiss a thousand new ways
whose hearts will be unafraid, outspoken
who i will try not, and fail, to measure against you
because in the museum of us
you are my Elizabeth Catlett
shaping a kind of nurturing
and pragmatic life
that has become my normal.

this is not the sad end of a love story
it is the beginning of a beautiful truth

sometimes i wish we weren't friends
that i had kneeled
before your delicate temple
grasped you in my full arms,
as we embraced into the morning

that i had put away those big
soft, dark friendly gestures and got close
got real close to you

but for now, i'll stick to awkward poems
and the precious memories
of your lofty smile
of a Goddess who loved me
wholly and solely.

INSTRUCTIONS FOR LEAVING

Once the earthquake is settled
accommodate the anger
let it move in, fix it dinner
then put it to bed.

Part as partners in wonder
stargazers discovering possibility
two people who dreamed a world
yesterday.

Keep a room in your heart
do not let your tomorrows explode
pay attention to memory
honor the knotty and the jubilant
the storm that felled you
but also, the rainbow.

Be neighborly
have less thunder in your mouth
make a joyful noise
do not waste time as rivals
erstwhile lovers who no longer laugh
play the new music of your life softly
like a sunrise mission.

Mourn the changing season
step out into what you have lost
and accomplished
have afternoon tea and
talk about it
remind each other
to leave something behind
that makes you smile.

Now, go be grateful.

PART FOUR

WHY FATHERS CRY AT NIGHT

I believe that what we become depends
on what our fathers teach us at odd
moments, when they aren't trying
to teach us. We are formed
by little scraps of wisdom.

—Umberto Eco

PORTRAIT OF TWO DAUGHTERS

Like the first words on a blank page
Like opening a handwritten letter
Like the last brushstroke on canvas

Like the choir *Moving on up a little higher*
Like the sermon ending and *Amen, Amen, Hallelujah!*
Like buying Sunday dinner at church

Like that feeling after a good meal
Like a sleeping dog at your foot
Like napping down by the riverside

Like the bounce on a last day of school
Like sandcastles on the beach
Like a cool drink of summer

You are irresistible
and I marvel
at the heavenly way
you light up my world

bring newness
to each thirsting day

This is what I know:
You are my Polaris
in this orbit
of fatherhood.

A COOL DRINK OF SUMMER
(CELEBRATION-SIZE)

Folks, when summer comes to town, you know that time of year when the kids are running around outside (or, at least they should be), there's nothing like a tall, cold glass of fruit punch. It will sweeten the day, for sure. This here is a simple, refreshing drink that's perfect for a summery gathering. Like a really good story, you know, the one with an extra-special twist at the end, feel free to swap the sparkling apple cider with your favorite bubbly. Yeah, baby!

I'm making this for a summer cookout most definitely. What I'm listening to is a bossa nova. Maybe Oscar Peterson's "Wave" or "Chega De Saudade" by Rosa Passos and Yo-Yo Ma.

TOTAL TIME: 30 MINUTES

MAKES: 8 1-CUP SERVINGS

CALORIES PER SERVING: 155

COURSE: BEVERAGE

Ingredients

1/3 gallon (about 5 cups) apple cider

1 bottle (24½ fluid ounces) sparkling white grape juice

2½ cups orange-mango juice

1 tablespoon freshly squeezed lime juice

Orange wedges

Instructions

In a large pitcher—or a great big ole jug—combine the cider and juices.

Float the orange wedges in the punch.

Chill in the fridge.

Serve well chilled—with muddled mint leaves in the glasses, if you like.

HOW WE MADE YOU

For Samayah

In the future
when you're newly married
and the two of you
are half hanging off your bed
fingers playing in each other's locks
your legs braided
loud garbage trucks beeping outdoors
no whining children yet to cook for
and you're talking about leaving your job
or whose family to visit for Christmas
or how lucky you are to be loved like this
or whatever it is you talk about
after making love in the early morning
I want you to know
that before our uncoupling
your mother and I used to work the door
at a jazz club in Washington, DC,
and every Thursday night we'd stand at the entrance

collecting covers
greeting friends and regulars
feeding each other jerk wings
kissing the hot sauce from our lips
joking and laughing about this and that
holding each other when it got chilly
and later when we'd get back to our one-room apartment
on the other side of the bridge
we'd spread the money out on the bed
count our haul
smile if we could pay the rent
worry if we couldn't
and then we'd make our own music
and without fail
the woman next door would bang on the walls
and tell us to turn it down
but we wouldn't
because we couldn't
because we knew how lucky we were
to be loved like that.

CONVERSATION BETWEEN
FATHER AND DAUGHTER

With Covid-19 came a house of horrors. I was afraid of bridges and heights, but those phobias were fleeting. While my then seventh-grade daughter, Samayah, stayed up until midnight and slept until noon, I dozed off soon after twilight only to be jolted awake by nightmares that I was dying.

If I thought the virus pandemic was a haunted house, then the racism pandemic was surely hell. Each unarmed Black man and woman removed from this earth at the hands and knees of white men hiding behind blue shields sent me spiraling into the abyss of terror.

We'd been living in London during all this and my daughter and I talked a great deal, but as I reflected on 2020, I wanted to know, directly, what she'd been reflecting on too.

So I asked her, starting with what she thought of the early days of sheltering in place.

For the first two months, I loved not being able to go outside, because I'm not a huge walker and you and Mom are. Every single day felt like summer vacation even though we still had distance learning. *So if you did have to wake up early, it would motivate you to finish your work early, and then I'd finish by lunchtime and have the rest of the day off to do whatever I wanted.*

Which was normally watch Disney+.

Very funny, Dad. One thing I did with you, which was one of the best things during lockdown, was I learned a new sport. I learned how to ride a skateboard and play softball—

At the same time?

I'm being serious. Like you said, you got to focus on your writing and I got to focus on new things I wanted to try out or finish old things that I started and never completed. So you and I playing catch, and me learning how to pitch, was a really fun experience, because I basically had all the time in the world to do it. And now that I'm a boss, all school sports have been canceled this fall. ARGH!

I think playing Frisbee and softball with you out in front of our flat was the absolute best for me, too. You know, before we were in lockdown, you'd go to school, you'd come home, and when I'd ask you how your day was, you'd mumble, "Fine." But softball was a time for us to spend quality time together. Kinda like how you and Mommy read books together at bedtime. I felt like this was our reading-books-together time that you and I got to do. And I thought you were really good at it. And I looked forward to it, because it meant a lot to me. I felt like we grew a lot closer.

Awww, that's special. We did get closer.

Even though it was a difficult year.

I watched the news and heard about the pandemic and it

scared me, and I wanted to go to the Black Lives Matter pro-
test, but you and Mom wouldn't let me because of Covid-19.
But as a middle school student, I was also focusing on school
and not being able to see my friends and not being able to have
a birthday party. I was tired of texting all day, every day. I
wanted to see them.

I thought it was really smart when you'd open the front
door of the flat and just sit in the chair and talk to your friends,
or do homework, or just stare outside.

I missed the real world.

I did too. I found that reading helped me stay in touch with
the world. I've never read so many books as I did during the
lockdown.

I realize that one of the good things about school is you get
to spend time with your friends without trying to think,
Hmmm, what should I say, what should we talk about, what's
really been going on with me?—which is what happens when
you don't have that human connection.

And, in the end, that's what it's all about. Connection,
really. Do we understand ourselves? Are we connected with
each other in a way that is life-giving and lifesaving?

Um, I guess, Dad.

[Laughs] Okay, so if you could pick something you learned
from this experience that you want to share with people—that
you learned about yourself, that you learned from the lock-
down—what would it be?

Since we had a lot more time to hang, and to be with our
family and parents and to really focus on ourselves, I learned
how to be way more grateful, because I saw all the things you

guys have to go through. I got to see all of your hard work liter-
ally every day, all day.

Well, that's a blessing. We should be locked down for the whole year! [Laughs] Seriously, that means a lot. I feel pretty cool now.

Ehhh ... pretty cool? I mean, you're cool adjacent, perhaps.

YOU'RE WELCOME

We got used to
the moonglow read-alouds
and the stars shining sing-alongs
the little lights of mine
and the Hogwarts gong
the cuddling
the dozing off
in your queen-size bed
the bad dreams
the crack of lightning
that led to you climbing in mine
the Thank you, Daddy,
for playing "Apples and Bananas"
the French toast at dinnertime
the dressing up in long gowns
the forgetting to brush
the occasional frown
the counting in Swahili
the school plays
the monkey bars
the long hugs
the way you cried
when Mommy left
for a weekend
or a lunch date

or a bath
We got used to those things.

But then the storm stopped bothering you
and your kisses were pithy
and your bed got smaller
and your door stayed shut
and Hermione was a feminist
and she wore Gucci
and your shorts got shorter
and your tops cropped higher
and your friends met you at the park
and you made up your own mind
and everything was just *Fine*
and *Doja Cat*
and your mother and I went for a walk
on the golden morning
you started high school
and we didn't say a word
we just watched
the yesterdays
of our Modern Family disappear
and I put my headphones on
and I listened to Raffi
and it started raining
like the sky was crying
and I became the sky
and the sun was saying
It's a new day, you're welcome.

TEN REASONS WHY FATHERS
CRY AT NIGHT

1. Because teenagers don't like park swings or long walks anymore unless you're in the mall.
2. Because holding her hand is forbidden and kisses are lethal.
3. Because school was "fine," her day was "fine," and yes, she's "fine." (So why is she weeping?)
4. Because you want to help, but you can't read minds.
5. Because she is in love and that's cute, until you find his note asking her to prove it.
6. Because she didn't prove it.
7. Because next week she is in love again and this time it's real, she says her heart is heavy.
8. Because she yearns to take long walks in the park with him.
9. Because you remember the myriad woes and wonders of spring desire.
10. Because with trepidation and thrill you watch your daughter who suddenly wants to swing all by herself.

PRELUDE TO LOVE

When you find yourself
face-to-face with a humdrum suitor — unflattered,
unmoved, midway through
smoked-fish butter curry,
coconut and roti
and all you can think about
is making a dash for the door
even though your tongue, your wanting palate pines
for the plum and juniper donuts
the restaurant is known for
I will be the dispatcher who calls
a car to take you, or better yet
I can drive you somewhere, anywhere
you want to go

When you meet the one
who takes you to Kehinde Wiley's *Prelude*
for a first date
then holds your hand and
carefully wipes your warm tears

after you've been punched
in the gut by the jarring way he paints
power and preclusion
I will be the maître d' who invites
the two of you to a private dinner
who serves old wine
and hellfire chili
who, when you go to the washroom, pulls
your suspicious lover
into my study
and offers the following thought:

I am no Michelangelo
I prefer blank verse
to mezza fresco.
She is my primo canvas
and you may marvel
all you want at her body
of work
as long as you remember
that she is the masterpiece
that colors our world
from floor
to ceiling.

And when, out of the blue, he asks
to take me fishing
or play a round of golf
I will arrive twenty minutes early

with tinted windows and
a smile, even though I don't like
golf, so I can see what kind of
confidence he parks with, he gets out
of his car with, he walks alone
with, and when we get to the boat
or on the green, I will,
with a deadly seriousness,
question your suspicious lover
about the unblinking execution
of postmodern politics
in the latest Percival Everett novel
and try not to laugh
to keep from crying.

What I am trying to say is
when you fall hard (and you will)
in love like a shooting star
I will be the soft ground
you remember
the sky full of memories
you look to
I will be the old man
sitting by the fire
picking you up with a lifetime
of lessons, tender stories of
longing and loss
that will never leave you
long after I have.

LOVE LESSON

The difference
between telling someone
you love them
and loving them
is the difference
between pumpkin
and sweet potato pie.

The difference
between loving
and being loved
is the difference
between watering a garden
and the autumn harvest.

SHE'S LEAVING HOME: AUGUST 18, 2009

Yesterday, on the long drive to campus, I kept looking in the rearview mirror. No one was tailgating me, there weren't any cops, and the road was empty, but for some reason I found myself glancing behind me more than usual. It occurred to me, a day later, that while we were surely headed forward, moving ahead, I found it soothing to look back on our past. Your eighteen years. I suppose that in life it is important to remember where you've been, as you move ahead. These are just a few of the things I remember about our past, young lady. Things that I hope you will carry with you—as lessons, as reminders, as guides.

I never went to college parties.

The first four years of your life, we lived in close to five different cities. You were a real trouper, adapting to the different areas and communities. And when your mother and I divorced, you handled it better than most children do. Better than I would have. In fact, when I was older than you, my parents announced that they were separating, and I cried and begged and pleaded for them to work it out. And they did. And if they hadn't I would have been destroyed. Nandi, since the beginning, you have been a strong woman. You bounce back. You manage expectations well. You adjust. You will need this during the next four years, as this is probably the biggest life change you will encounter. So embrace it. Run circles around yet another city in your life. Keep doing what you've been doing since you were a baby. Adapt. Be determined.

Of course, I know you are sensitive, and I know that even though you've handled lots of challenges in your life brilliantly, you keep some things inside. A little of that is okay. A lot, not so okay. Nandi, if you ever feel like the pieces of the puzzle don't fit, your world is too unpleasant, and the sky is crashing, talk to someone. Talk to me. Talk to your God. Talk to your teacher. Talk to the girl at Starbucks. Talk to a therapist. Talk to someone. See, sometimes, sharing offers focus, and listening is an act of love that can renew your spirit.

One month into your mother's pregnancy, I saw you in a dream. Vividly. I saw your nose, eyes, skin. You were as clear as springwater. I was twenty-two, with no idea how to be a father, and a little afraid I might not figure it out. But after the dream, I was thrilled, ecstatic, over the moon about your joining us. Eight months later, in the delivery room, I guess I went overboard, videotaping the whole thing. I was just so filled with joy at the opportunity to meet and help raise you. I told myself that when you went to college, I would let you watch the video. I thought it would be one of those movie moments that we could share together. Well, I went back to look at a little of it, and I stopped after a few seconds. I realized that this is one of those rare moments in our history that I want to remember as is. Knowing is great, but I'd rather hold on to the feeling. (Plus, I didn't remember it being so, uh, messy.)

After the divorce, you came to stay with me every other weekend. Back in those days, as a starving artist, I didn't have a lot of material things. I had a few books, poems, and lots of love for you. Whenever you'd come visit, you'd always say things like *I like your hat, Daddy,* or *I like your coat, Daddy,* and it made me feel on top of the world. I thank you for that. Nandi, as you encounter people in life, whether it's your professor or the person mowing the lawn, your roommate or the cafeteria aide, always share positive sentiments with them. You don't know what's going on in their life, good or bad, but a few wonderful words can make someone feel brighter, can make a lonely poet forget about the bus fare he doesn't have.

FYI, I never went to parties in college. I studied all the time.

Speaking of college, junior year I took a sociology class. I loved the class. And the teacher. I just never went to class. I did the papers—on issues that I was interested in. And skipped the tests. I flunked the final. Now, when grades came, I was totally expecting an F. It just so happened, that junior year was my "radical" year. It was the year I organized antiapartheid rallies on campus, held protests in the snow, and generally worked day and night to make conditions better for minority groups. Translation: I was very active on campus, just not attending too many classes. So when the grades came out, my sociology professor had given me a C+. He explained that while most of the students were learning about *Minority Group Relations* in his class, I was out in the real world learning about it and putting it into practice. And he admired that. Okay, first, I am not saying you should skip classes. That would be a mistake (and I would have to cut off your allowance — SMILE), but I think college is about learning in and out of the classroom. Become involved, Nandi. Bridge that gap between knowledge and experience.

I went to one party in college. It was a local weekly dance contest, at the Marriott. Started at eleven o'clock on Friday nights. I'd won a couple Fridays, and your uncle Marshall won a few Fridays also. One Friday night they had the final competition, and Marshall and I and our partners went head-to-head. I should have won, but Marshall started doing some combination of the Reebok and the Jerk (Google it). And losing was a terrible experience for me. Which is the point, that if you never go to parties and dance contests, Nandi, you will never lose. So don't go to any parties.

Honesty. Rule #1 in life. Never lie. (Unless you're telling your first child you didn't go to parties in college. That is okay.) Your reputation is how folks know and respect you, Nandi. First and foremost, be an honest and trustworthy person, and not only will others feel good about you, but you will feel good about yourself. Speaking of which, please sign the form that says I can view your grades at the end of each semester.

Friendship. Rule #2 in life. You attract what you are. When you look in your rearview mirror, do you see the kinds of friendships that will last a lifetime? I suspect not. College is a place where all that changes. My best friend in life, the guy who beat me in the dance contest, I met on the first day of college. If you want to meet good, honest, caring, friendly people, then be good, honest, caring, and friendly from day one. It's as simple as that.

Here are some of the highlights of life with you, my dear:

The day you were born.

The day you bit the boy in preschool.

The day my first book came out, with our photo on the cover.

The day we sat outside in 100-degree weather selling copies of my first book.

The day you won the MLK historical essay contest.

The day you walked down the aisle at my wedding.

The day you announced you wanted to be a poet.

The day you started high school.

The day you started varsity volleyball as a freshman.

The day you turned sixteen and I showed up in the limo.

The day you came to live with me.

The day during your junior year when you told us "I got this, school will be fine."

The day you opened the letter from NYU and it said you got a full scholarship to the Summer Program.

The day you watched Samayah for the first time. And didn't drop her.

The day you graduated cum laude.

The day you got offered the full scholarship to college.

The day I got the bill for $0.

The day you walked up the hill to your dorm and never looked back.

So here we are, eighteen years after The Dream. And I find myself wanting to say something deep. To offer some glimpse of what the future will hold for you, Nandi. And the reality is, you don't need me to tell you what the future will hold, any more than you needed me to videotape your birth. I'm the one looking back, trying to remember. You're on your way up the hill. In the dorm, up the stairs, to room 218. Looking forward. "I got this, Dad" is what I hear, and I believe that you do. I guess this is more about me. Wasn't it just a minute ago when we were walking to the tennis courts in Ashland, or swinging in the park in Norfolk, or singing some of our favorite made-up songs? Geesh, Nandi, I miss you already! I miss the drama and your dynamic charm. I miss your attitude and your attention to family. I miss your fiery personality (just a little) and your focus on excellence. I know you're not gone, you're just in another city, and now I must learn to adapt and adjust. Be pertinacious. Don't worry, though, "I think I got this..."

PS. Your mother never partied either.

I LIKE YOUR

I like my shoes when they are with
your shoes. Mostly the comes. Leastly
your goes. I carry your footsteps(onetwothreefour)
in between today . . . tomorrow.
Again
     and again
          and again
             I like
to feel the flowers
and the follow
to your lead
It is such a happy thing to yes the next with you
to walk on magic love rugs beneath the what
and why nots
the anythings of
liking everybloomingthing—four feet, two hearts, one
great   GREAT   GREAT(US)

going.

LAMENT

Every night since you disappeared
I hop in the car
and take an aimless ride
like we used to do when you were two
and wouldn't sleep

I wheel through the city
passing parks and foggy cemeteries
seeking a sliver of memory

I park sometimes at our late-night grocer
watching the nurse whose shift just ended
get a box of eggs
an inexpensive claret
because she lives alone
and wants breakfast for dinner

watching the guy who's just been laid off
get a lottery ticket
and construction paper
because his seventh grader
waited till the last minute

Time is not a trusted lover
The seconds, the months will break us, like petals
Silence is our enemy

So I just sit here
playing your favorite song
and when it ends
I play it again

Things have come to this

Me dying a little inside
the darkness growing so heavy
we can no longer see each other

Me hoping the sun will arrive
before it is too late.

Me finally falling asleep
dreaming of our shared world
waking up
a father
again.

A LETTER TO NANDI

When we last spoke
you were traveling for work
but you couldn't tell me where

you were traveling
for special, sensitive work
in the Navy

a giant destroyer ship
built for special warfare
takes three years of work

I wonder what you have built
in the three years since we last spoke
since this war has nearly destroyed me.

I wonder do I have a grandchild?
Is he sensitive?
Have you taught her how to swim, like I taught you?

The weight of not knowing
you anymore is a heavy blues,
a giant ship bearing down

on my precious heart
You were my true north
But I am off course since we last spoke

Everything is in pieces, dismantled
I cannot get my bearings
I even bought a special navy-blue compass

to point me in the right direction
It took 100,000 ancient Egyptians twenty years
to build the Great Pyramid at Giza

How many does it take to rebuild a love
that has traveled so far apart,
that is nearly drowning?

There are nearly twenty years between us
I wonder if we can assemble
enough precious memory

to forgive
before it weighs too much
before our time is destroyed

I am waving a white flag
I am pleading the grand Sun
to point me toward

the pyramid
that was you, me, us
my true north

once again.

PORTRAIT OF A FATHER

I am the father of two daughters. One, freshly planted in high school with big Hollywood dreams and a post-Covid anxiety that amped up her already-justified stressful reaction to her parents' separation; the other newly thirty, her career blossoming. The teenager informed me that she simply didn't have the energy to talk with me after a long day spent talking to friends and teachers and coaches and her advisor and...that if I wanted to engage with her, I would need to take her to school in the mornings so we could chat, rather than make her use public transportation. She kept her word. The other daughter, who came to live with me at fifteen, a quiet, consistently kind, altruistic, reliable, and industrious woman, told me, in the middle of a familial disagreement—one of only a few heated arguments we've ever had—that she would never speak to me again. It's been three years, and she is immovable. At night, I sit in the dark, in the space between hope and heart, the grief stealing warmth, trying to remember how to love, trying to figure out the right words to bring you both back to me. Without branches, a tree cannot produce anything...because there is nowhere to grow. There are mornings when I wonder if I am still a father. On those days, I read my journal, sitting between the laughter, trying to remember us, like we were, before.

October 13, 2010

I just spent fifteen glorious minutes cutting a peanut butter sandwich into four perfect parallelograms because the two-year-old will only eat them if they are cut in parallelograms. I tried to trick her and made one a square, to which she replied, "That's not a paroyellowglam."

March 16, 2011

I have two daughters: a twenty-year-old, and a two-year-old. They are the world that i live in. They are the love that owns me. They are tulips in my garden: sweet, showy, and full of color. They are my dreams. come. true.

May 5, 2011

The two-year-old didn't want to go to Montessori today. In the car, on the way to school, she starts singing "Swing Low, Sweet Chariot" all loud and whatnot. Like she was Harriet Tubman, and I was trying to keep her from her freedom.

June 29, 2011

The two-year-old just got put into time-out by the mother. Now she's crying, calling my name, to come rescue her. So, naturally, I'm walking in her room to soothe her, when I come upon the mother. Now I'm in time-out.

June 16, 2012

This from the daughter who is studying abroad in Italy: "I LOVE YOU SO MUCH! You have been there for me through good and bad. I really am thankful and blessed that you helped me make this study abroad experience happen for me. You are amazing not only to me but also to my sister. Thank you for being a father and doing all that you can for your daughters. P.S. please put $100 in my account. I am kinda broke. It would be greatly appreciated."

June 29, 2012

Your mom just called: I'm proud of you & all the good work that you are doing. I really did a good job raising you, but I do want to apologize for all the spankings.

We learn how to parent by watching and listening to our parents and the adults in our extended community. Growing up, your grandfather never said *I love you*. He wasn't the verbally-express-your-emotions kind of person. Wait, that's not true. He expressed himself A LOT, it's just that he chose anger and shouting rather than trying a little tenderness. I don't have fond memories of father-son bonding time in my adolescent years. There were no hot-dogs-and-cotton-candy autumns. Because there were no baseball games. He was a round-the-clock entrepreneur.

Home was serious business with little time for little things like card games and Ping-Pong and talking. He also traveled a lot, and even though I was relieved to have a break from his temper, from his overbearing, bookish sagacity, I missed the possibility of us.

When I think of how I knew this man actually loved me, I remember a thing he would do. Every Sunday, after his sermon ended and the pews emptied, I would walk up to the pulpit, shadow his stillness, hope for some movement on this desert island, look up into blinding sun, sweat clinging to a high mountain. His face, a golden moon, would beam, and his hands would massage my scalp, like spring rain drizzling earth. I guess it's why I love saying *I love you*, and from time to time, even though I know not to touch a Black woman's hair, you let me rub my fingers through your braids. It's me reminding myself of the little bricks that make up the architecture of a relationship. It's me remembering how to love, and showing it.

March 2, 2012

BEFORE: Whenever I'm heading out for travel/ work, the three-and-a-half-year-old attaches herself to my leg and hollers that she does not want her daddy to leave her. This is the worst part of doing the job that I love; and I simply can't take her with me every time. So, recently I've started a new ritual: I went to Target and purchased a ton of those one-dollar trinkets (stickers, books, cups, bubbles, games, etc.), and each time I leave for work, I give her wrapped gifts totaling the number of days that I will be gone. So, if I'm gone for three days, she gets three gifts, etc. And she can only open one gift per day. The first time, it worked wonderfully, she didn't holler when she held on to my leg. The second time, no leg grabbing.

AFTER: Last night, I left to speak at a conference in New York. I would be gone for one day, so I gave her ONE quickly wrapped gift. As I headed out the door, she looked at me and said, Daddy, when are you gonna be gone ten days, and then she kissed me goodbye.

March 5, 2012

Yesterday, I tell the three-and-a-half-year-old we are going to buy some school supplies and toys for the children of Konko, a village I'll be visiting in the eastern region of Ghana. She immediately starts asking me what toy I will get for her. I explain that she won't be getting anything, and that she should remember all the wonderful gifts she received for her birthday. She then starts whining about how she should be able to get something like the village kids. So I pick up two dolls from the shelf and tell her we are having a puppet show. She perks up then. I proceed to stage a two-doll show, right there in the middle of Target, about a little girl who has nine soccer balls, and another little girl who has none. It is a moving tale (okay, maybe not, but she thinks so). At the end of the story, I ask her what should be done about the girl who has no ball. She replies, "We can give her one of our balls. Or maybe we can buy her one." The whining stops, and we set off on our journey. At each store, she lets the cashier know that we are buying for kids in Ghana who don't have balls like we do. She even makes me buy a flaming-red soccer ball, because she claims the kids won't want a plain white one. Also, lots of bubbles.

April 7, 2012

In the mornings, like her older sister, the three-and-a-half-year-old can be a little ornery. So this morning, when she comes down the stairs, I put on this song, and I start dancing. She looks at me like I've lost it, but then her head starts twitching, and her feet start jiggling; then she starts throwing her hands in the air (and waving like she just don't care), and before long we're both grinning and dancing around the living room, like we're in the audience of The Ellen Show *or something.*

April 27, 2012

What I didn't tell you is that when we do our morning dance the little one dances like Elaine on Seinfeld.

July 21, 2012

Heading to Panera this morning to work on the new book, the nearly four-year-old asks me, "When are you going to work, Daddy." I respond, "In fact, I am going to work now." "You are? What work?" she asks. "To write a book. You know, that's what Daddy does." "To write a book for me?" "Yes, darling, for you and a lot of other people." "Your work is to write a book, Daddy?" "Indeed it is." After a few minutes of pondering, she says, "Mom, did you know that Daddy works at Panera Bread?"

August 21, 2012

Today is my birthday. Both of my daughters celebrated with me. Cake, ice cream, and lots of hugs. The twenty-one-year-old took the four-year-old to Chuck E. Cheese while I read and napped. It was the best present ever. To watch two feisty, assured, loving daughters become who they are under my watchful eye, inside the air that gives me life. And what a precious life it is.

I also learned how to father from men who failed miserably. The friend of my father's who got into a violent argument with his wife in my grandmother's driveway and, upon being chased by a knife-wielding woman, proceeded to lift his seven-year-old daughter, my best friend, in front of him as a shield. A college friend's father who'd been sentenced to prison for abusing troubled teenagers during his kid's sleepovers. An old girlfriend's father who lived around the corner her entire childhood and never once came over to see her, who never invited her to his house, who refused to acknowledge her, even when she walked past his house, a monsoon of heartbreak forming behind her juvenile eyes. I wasn't any of these men, and I would never be, but I carried the weight of their failures with my own insecurities as a father. I would be the dad who protected, who you could always count on, who not only acknowledged you but exalted you, who lifted you up in all of your majesty, who reassured you, who carried your heart in my heart. I would be a father who held on to you, shared what little wisdom I'd collected from those before me, then let you go off into the world and discover its wonder. You not coming back was never the plan. Is unimaginable. A tree with no branches.

November 7, 2013
    Why I stood, arms folded, for 25 minutes. At FIVE A.M. THIS MORNING:

Me (dreaming about a cupcake and a frog): zzzzzzzzzzzz
Her (jumping on my bed): Dad, what does Georgia 'Keeffe look like?
Me: ARRGGGGGGH!
Her: Dad, I'm doing a pain'ing.
Me: Daddy's sleeping.
Her: It's gonna be a po'tr'it.
Me (yawning): Oh right, you're studying artists in school? Jacob Lawrence?
Her: Dad, that was last year. It's van Gogh.
Me: Yeah, van Gogh. (Pronunciation: Van Go)
Her: No, it's van Gogh. (Pronunciation: Vohn Goughfh-houhh$&$&&)
Me: Bless you. He did the water lilies, right?
Her: Claude Monet, Dad. Geesh.
Me (turning over, pulling covers up): Daddy's still sleeping, honey.
Her (pulling covers down): I need your help. Meet me in my studio [room] NOW, please.
Me: ARGGGGGHHH! Fine.

Her (in studio): Okay, I'm going to do an impression of you, like Mary Cassatt.

Me (on her bed under covers): Okay, great!

Her: You can't lay down, Dad. You have to stand up for the painting.

Me: Fine. How long?

Her: Until I finish the sketch. Then you can text or email or do whatever you want while I color. Now, I need you to stand over there with your arms crossed looking straight ahead, please.

Me (standing with my arms crossed looking straight ahead).

Her: Dad, please look interesting.

25 minutes later . . .

Her: Finished.

Me (looking at the drawing): Hmm, that's an abstract, right?

Her: Nope, it's definitely a po'tr'it. What do you think, Dad?

Me (smiling): It's absolutely brilliant.

In this portrait of fatherhood, I am not close to perfect. In this forest of parenthood, I am winding my way through a lifetime of lessons, finding faith in a jubilant sea of memory. Longing for the wonder of one daughter's daybreak, while trying to water the new seed bursting in another one's extraordinary promise. In this portrait of fatherhood, know that:

what matters is you
you, you, you, you, you, you
then everything else.

I am a father of two daughters. I have walked in the joy of their golden feet. And sometimes stumbled off the mountain of their precious hearts. The song we sing together makes a joyful noise, which can sometimes sound like the weary blues. But know this: if the trees can keep dancing, so can we.

PART FIVE

A LETTER TO MY MOTHER

All anyone can hope for is just a tiny bit of love,
like a drop in a cup if you can get it, or a waterfall,
a flood, if you can get that too.

—Edwidge Danticat, *Krik? Krak!*

REBOUND

I made myself a promise not to conduct any business, other than rewriting a novel (I was under a book deadline, you see) during the vacation, so I turned off my cell phone and took a breather for the first time in three years. I'd been on the road, visiting hundreds of schools around the world, reading poetry, autographing books (and arms and sneakers and . . .), and surprising students who'd discovered the joys of reading after finishing one of my books. As we cruised along the Inside Passage from Vancouver to Alaska, I was determined to log out of my writerly life and spend my time reading the latest Elmore Leonard, fine-tuning a chapter here and there, watching live musicals with my nine-year-old, or napping. Mostly napping.

Having decided in advance that the family would need to unwind from our very cold Disney Alaskan Cruise, after we docked we headed for part two of our holiday—a sunnier week at the tranquil and plush Chrysalis Inn and Spa in Bellingham, Washington. The only reason I turned on my phone then was because it was my birthday.

There were three voice mail messages. The first was from my mother singing "Happy Birthday" and saying August twenty-first was the best day of her life (I'm sure she told each of her children the same thing about their birth dates). The second was from a bill collector. And the third was from my father, saying very calmly, *Hey, your mother checked herself out of the hospital.* This was news to me because I didn't know she was *in* the hospital.

We flew home a few days later, sped the three-and-a-half-hour drive to Chesapeake, Virginia, and when I pulled up, there was an ambulance parked in front of her building, and a lot of commotion going on beside it. I greeted my siblings and father, who were engaged in a heated exchange about whether they should avoid "Western" medicine and just take her back upstairs—an argument that caused so much ruckus that many other residents of the community began to gather ringside as if at a boxing match—then immediately walked over to the EMTs to inquire what was going on. When they confirmed who I was, they escorted me into the back of the ambulance, where I found, lying on a gurney, the woman who brought me into this world. She looked at me and I didn't even recognize her. Her face was sunken, she was smaller, thinner, but she smiled, which relieved me. Then uttered the words that would haunt me, *I don't want any of them to come to the hospital, only you.*

After *The Crossover* won the 2015 Newbery Medal, an annual award given since 1922 for the most outstanding contribution to American literature for children, the pressure was on to write more books. From my publisher. From me. From the thousands of students I saw each month at my author visits, who pleaded for a sequel. While I didn't then see what the future of twin brothers Josh and JB looked like, I was intrigued by the idea of delving into their father, Chuck's, past. So I signed a contract to write a prequel. *Rebound.* And I promised to deliver the book to my publisher in January 2017. Yes, a plan.

January 2017 came and went. No book delivered. The best-laid plans…

The book deadline was extended to March 2017, and when that date also came and fled, my publisher had what the old folks would call a *Come to Jesus* talk with me. It seemed the book had a schedule that needed to be adhered to in order for all of the many departments involved with bookmaking—editorial, design, printing, marketing, sales—to do their jobs efficiently and brilliantly. I was interfering with that plan, and so I could set one final deadline that I needed to keep to. *July 1, 2017,* I said to the powers that be, after I reminded them, with a smirk on my face, that I'd won a Newbery and you can't rush genius. I was only a quarter joking. I fully expected to finish in plenty of time and restore their faith in my writerly professionalism. I failed.

The final deadline I was given, *or there'd be problems, Kwame,* was September 1, 2017. Each morning on the cruise ship, I'd spend a few hours on deck with my laptop, then turn it off and visit the spa, or take a gold rush excursion, or engage in the bliss of nothingness. When I got the call from my father, I was nearly finished, with maybe another thirty pages to go before I pressed send.

There was one recliner, large, brown leather, in her hospital room. This worked out, because I was the only one with her. We talked, ate a little, watched television, then she fell asleep and I worked on the book, because it was due in five days.

The next morning, the doctors said they were giving her antibiotics and medicines to help. To help what, I asked. It seemed that she had fluid in her lungs, and her diabetes was worse, that kidney failure was imminent, but they were doing everything they needed to do, so not to worry. Telling a son not to worry about his sickly mother is fruitless. I worried. And while she slept, I worked on the book, because it was due in four days.

On the third day, she still refused to allow anyone but me to be there. Her big brother came anyway. They held hands, said a prayer, then she looked up at him, like I'm sure she'd done many times as a child, hoping that he'd protect her, look out for her, and told him, *It's in God's hands now, Bobby.* I sat in the recliner, listening to their tender words, and working on the book, because it was due in three days.

The next day was a blur. I woke up to my mother having a stroke. Her eyes were still open, but she could no longer talk, move, eat. I guess, just fed up at not being able to do anything for herself, she closed her eyes and slept. Or so I thought. I called my siblings and my father and they came to the hospital and sat with me. And watched her. She'd occasionally open her eyes and stare at them. I sat back worried and wondering if she was in pain, and I worked on the book, because it was due in two days.

My father stayed overnight with her. It was the first night I wasn't with her. It was a cruel foreshadowing. I rushed back to the hospital at dawn, only to have the doctors tell me there was nothing they could do for my mother, that she was alive because of the breathing machine. I was alive because of her. What would happen when she was no longer?

My sisters and I talked and agreed to take her home. If she was going to die, I thought, let it be in the privacy and comfort of her own bed. But first, I'd need to ask her permission. I said a quick prayer that I would find the right words, that this writer would be able to use his words in this moment of unprecedented anguish, then I grabbed her hand, whispered in her ear, *You can go now, woman, I got you. I got this. I'll take care of them all*, and that's when it hit me. She didn't want her two daughters and her husband in the hospital room with her because she was angry with them for all the drama and unhelpful energy they would bring to her hospital room; she didn't want them there because she was still protecting them, still mothering them, still loving them in the same way that she did when she'd wake up at five on icy December mornings when our gas heater was broken, to gather wood for the fireplace, and put beach towels in the dryer until they were burning hot so that we could wrap them around us after our baths. She was always thinking of others. Even on her deathbed. So why did she want me there is the question I asked myself, as I sat in the recliner working on the book, because it was due in one day.

We took her home on September 1, 2017, in the evening, around five o'clock.

We took her home, and I proceeded to meet with hospice and coordinate the daily schedule.

We took her to her bed, placed her in it, and my sister climbed in and lay with her.

We took her home, and at 8:30 p.m., my mother, cradled in my sister's arms, crossed over to what I can only hope is a new world of dominoes and turkey legs and poetry and family, and I finished the book. I finished the book that I'd been missing deadlines on for nearly a year. The book that Arielle and Margaret, my concerned agent and editor, had instructed me days before to forget about, to stop writing so that I could focus on my mother, the love of my life.

She went home, and I think I had to finish writing the book to start the process of being okay with that. I had to finish writing *that book*, about a boy who was learning how to rebound on the court, and off, when his father dies, because I was going to have to rebound from the most devastating thing I'd ever experienced in my now forty-nine years. None of us is ever prepared for death. Writing helped me face it. I used my words, Barbara.

I used my words. Thank you.

MISSED CALL: JULY 18, 2017, 6:41 P.M.

The B&W of our birthday celebration in Howard
    Johnson's
The Polaroid of me in your arms blowing out the candles
The moldy Mickey Mouse ears from Disney World
Your charcoal gray, nineteen-inch Samsonite suitcase
The wood diploma frame of your Columbia master's
    degree
The videotape of you performing African folktales
The scotch-taped handmade bamboo rainstick that I broke
The round Pyrex casserole dish that I still bake in
The paisley chaise lounge in the basement that I still sit on
Your favorite J. California Cooper novel
The 1962 Drifters album
The starry van Gogh in the cheap frame
Your mother's chipped mahogany coffee table
"The Beautiful Girl Who Had No Teeth" recording
The cluster of brown moles under my eyes
That infectious smile
The memory of your pastalia
The memory of watching you cook

while you and Ben E. King sang
"Save the Last Dance for Me"
and your ashes, your life remains
in the hand-painted Moroccan ceramic jar
above the fireplace
in the family room
are all the things you left me
the keepsakes I think of
each time I listen
to your voice mail message:
Hey, Kwame.
Call me back.
Bye.

PASTALIAS

This is what my sisters and I called them. My mother's savory golden pastries filled with tasty ground beef that she served us as snacks on lucky summer afternoons. She never wrote down the recipe, and the closest thing I've been able to find that resembled it on the internets is a thing called *Pastelitos de Carne*. A Cuban pastry that literally translates as small cake filled with beef. Of all my mother's dishes I've prepared over the years, I've never made this one. In fact, I hadn't even remembered it until I was living in London and teaching myself to cook. And writing this book. Still, it took me being back in America to even attempt it. I remember it being a little flaky, really soft, not too spicy and simply delicious. I've changed a few things, according to my own palate and diet — added tomato paste to give it a sauce (hers was all meat filling), midafternoon snack, I'm pretty sure she made her own dough (I didn't), I'm pretty sure she didn't use chili powder or cayenne because we would have complained it was TOO SPICY, and I substituted ground turkey for the beef (which is why I added the sage, because it gives it a more meaty flavor). I've only made this afternoon snack once, and the truth is, it wasn't great. Eating them, I could taste hints of my mother's dish, but I definitely wouldn't serve it at a dinner party. Yet. The pastry is too sweet (Nex time, I'll make my own). I got the seasonings right, but the sauce is either overpowering or is underwhelming. I guess I look at my recipe, like I think of you reading this book. It's a start. You've got something to build on. I may not ever perfect it, but I'm still growing as a cook. And a lover. And making this dish is a reminder that there's room for a whole heaping lot of growth.

What I'm listening to while I bake: "Almost Like Being in Love" by Eydie Gormé.

TOTAL TIME: 45 MINUTES

MAKES: 12 SERVINGS

CALORIES PER SERVING: 250

COURSE: APPETIZER

Ingredients

1 package of pie crust or puff pastry

8 oz. ground turkey

1 tbsp. olive oil

1 egg for egg wash

1 onion medium, diced

2 cloves garlic minced

1 ½ tsp. Kosher salt

1 tsp. sage

1/4 tsp. chili powder

1 1/2 tbsp. cilantro

¼ tsp. cayenne pepper

¼ tsp. cumin

1/8 nutmeg

1 tsp. tomato paste

Instructions

Preheat oven to 400 degrees.

Heat oil on medium-high in a skillet. Sauté onions, and garlic for three minutes, then add the ground turkey and break down into small pieces.

Add salt, sage, cayenne, chili powder, cumin, and nutmeg.

Continue to cook until meat is thoroughly cooked. Stir in the tomato paste and blend well.

Finally stir in the cilantro.

Line a baking sheet with parchment paper.

Place pastry sheets on a lightly floured surface. Using a 3" biscuit cutter (or rim of a glass) cut circles. You will end up with 9-12 circles.

Place a heaping teaspoon of meat in the center of 9 of the circles. Using a pastry brush, brush egg wash around the perimeter of each circle.

Place the empty round on top, and using the tines of a fork press the edges firmly together.

Brush top with egg wash, place on baking sheet, and bake for about 12-15 minutes or until golden brown.

PORTRAIT OF A MOTHER AND SON

Remember in the hospital room when your lungs stopped behaving...and the doctor asked if I wanted to shut off the machine...the one loaning you breath...and I asked if you wanted to go home...to die...in your bed...and you squeezed my hand...once for yes...There was this moment...where I saw in your face...a smile the size of a planet...a woman lifting her lavender dress...walking into the water...unburdened... arriving at herself...smelling of honeysuckle...naked with happiness...and even though I'd been the one to ask the question...I was not prepared for your answer...for the drowning sadness...that has owned me ever since.

There are answers I still need...How you made a fire... pancakes...got four kids bathed and ready...each morning... Founded a school...Spent real time with your parents twice a week...Cooked an entrée and two sides...for six people... every evening...stayed when he strayed...still believed in love...wholly and solely...and danced joyfully around the house...like the sea was a part of your body...I've always wondered if you ever cried at night...long after we were dreaming...a world.

Now, you are gone...and I've carried your ashes...from one country to another...like luggage that I can't unpack...like little North Stars I cannot touch...I have come to a crossroads...no longer wanting to suffocate...waiting to exhale...trying to find my own answers...the right words...to say goodbye...to thank you for leaving me...with some soul to keep...to finally let go...of your hand...to go home...to live...to love...anew.

PART SIX

CODA

CONVERSATION WITH MYSELF

Well, you did *that*, sir.

I've had a lot of love in my life.

And you've honored it here, well. You are a master at learning to love. Thanks to all who helped make you.

Wait, are you being sarcastic?

Remember what your therapist said, "You haven't been single since 1987." Which means you haven't known what it means to survive the ache and anxiety of transforming from an immature manchild to adult man . . . alone.

So not true. I am a grown man who has lived through two divorces and the death of the most important woman in the world.

You've relied on the women in your life to mother you—

That's what women are supposed to do!

Supposed to do? I hope that's *you* being sarcastic, now. Look, all I'm saying is, in many ways because of the nurturing of Mommy and Granny and Stephanie and Pam and Nandi and Samayah and Sia and Nataki and Beatrice and Nikki—

Okay, is this really necessary?

We are better for their love, but in one particular way, you are not.

I love how it's WE when it's positive, and ME when it's not.

This isn't about good and bad. It's about asking the right questions, so you can start answering them, so you can begin building a true monument of love.

Look, I never said I was perfect. In fact, I said writing this book was all about my imperfections... A window into the darkness of doubt and the unbearable lightness of being in love... A putting back together... A carrying on... Snapshots of a man learning to love. Again.

Maybe now you can learn to love yourself.

Okay, that's not fair.

You don't know what it means to exist outside of love. You haven't had to be responsible for just you, accountable to your own metamorphosis.

Stop being so dramatic.

Okay, let me say it a different way. Being alone with yourself doesn't mean you will be lonely.

And, I haven't been able to separate the two?

Remember what Mommy used to say to you? When you'd bust into our sisters' room and beg them to stop whatever they were doing? And just play with you?

Mommy would say, "Kwame, why can't you just leave them alone and be by yourself?

"The world is a difficult place to live in and distraction is the name of the game."

Now you're quoting Toni Morrison.

Well, you don't listen to me. So maybe you'll listen to Toni. You love to say how much in love you are with *love*, but the one person you should love, you avoid.

Okay, so now you trying to say I don't love who I am. That's just crazy.

I'm saying that the difference between loving who you are and loving YOU is the difference

between pumpkin and sweet potato pie.

I literally just wrote a whole book examining my life, my loves, all my foils and foibles, my dreams and desires. I've never been so real, so raw. I'm not completely clueless, you know.

"Those who do not weep, do not see."

I don't know that one, but enough with the quotes already.

Victor Hugo (*Les Misérables*).

Right. Whatever. Stop alluding and implying and just say what you mean. What else am I doing wrong?

Do you remember when Mommy died?

September 1, 2017.

Do you remember when you cried?

Um, I didn't really cry—

Think maybe we should have?

If you hadn't interrupted me, you would have heard me say, Yet! I haven't cried yet.

What are you waiting for, it's been six years.

. . .

And do you remember when you knew your twenty-year marriage was over?

Yes.

Have you grieved?

What do you mean?

Divorce is a kind of slow death.

. . .

Do you remember that day three years ago when your first-born told you she never wanted to see you again?

. . .

Isn't it ironic what you chose to title this book? And yet, you haven't really.

Well, I definitely want to cry now.

Distractions often keep us from dealing with the ache and the hurt. From feeling and shedding the intense sadness and the uncertainty. Which keeps us from the healing. One of my friends recently told me: *Healing is worth the work.*

I hear you. Perhaps, that's what this book is. Part of the work.

I'm proud of you for writing it. I think our daughters will appreciate it in the future, as a glimpse into who you were, how you became the man you are, and ultimately, evolved into the man you are becoming. But the truth of the matter is this book isn't solely for them. Or for Mommy, who will never read it—

Too soon, man.

You wrote this book as a nudge to yourself.

To be single?

To be by yourself. And remind yourself that being alone is not the same as being lonely. You know it's time.

I do.

It's time to really take stock of your longing and loss. To do a full inventory on all the matters of your heart. To fall in love—

With myself.

By yourself.

But, what about falling in love. And sex, and all those things that I am now an expert at.

You should title the next installment, *Why Father's Laugh in the Morning,* 'cause your humor game is on point.

So, what's next?

You tell me.

I think I'm going to spend more time alone. And have more conversations with myself. Alone while I mourn the passing of the first woman I loved. Alone while I sit inside the tombstone of my marriage, I—

Great idea, but do me a favor and stop hiding behind all the metaphors. I know you're a poet and all. And try to allow yourself the time and space not just to be alone, but also, to grieve?

I will grieve. The guilt of ending my marriage. The feeling that I have betrayed my family. The ruptured relationship with my eldest child. The realization that my youngest child is becoming a young woman and will soon leave the nest. I will sit by myself and with myself until I get to know all of me. For as long as it takes. No matter how hard it is. And I will survive it.

Yes, you will survive it. And, she will come back to us

Someone recently told me something. Words of wisdom that will be helpful on my journey. She said—

She?! C'mon, man. You *just* said you were going to be alone…

No, no. Not like that. She's just a friend. And she said, "Kwame, you are not a grown man. You are a growing man."

A "growing" man. I like that. And you know what?

What?

I'm proud of you for growing. I'm proud of you for choosing you.

You know what else?

What?

Me too.

EPILOGUE

As a father, I certainly have a better understanding and a bit more compassion with regards to not only why certain questions are difficult to ask our fathers but also, why fathers aren't always forthcoming. What I've learned and continue to learn, and what I share in this memoir, is the realization that fatherhood, much like everything else in life, is often a beautiful mess. There are things in this book I probably should have told my wife before I told the world. There are love notes and petitions to my daughters that maybe should have been shared face-to-face. There are conversations I didn't have with my father before this book was written and while it was being written. Ironically, this book, in a way, forced me to have ALL of those hard talks. And I am so better for it. That's what I want this book to spark—those difficult but necessary conversations that ultimately make us better. With our loved ones and with ourselves. Ain't life grand!

ABOUT THE AUTHOR

Kwame Alexander is the number one *New York Times* bestselling author of 38 books, including *The Door of No Return, Light for the Worlds to See: A Thousand Words on Race and Hope, Becoming Muhammad Ali* (co-authored with James Patterson), *An American Story* (illustrated by Dare Coulter) *The Undefeated* (illustrated by Kadir Nelson), *Out of Wonder: Poems Celebrating Poets* (ed. with Marjory Wenworth and Chris Colderley), and his Newbery medal–winning novel, *The Crossover*. A regular contributor to NPR's Morning Edition, Kwame is the recipient of numerous awards, including The Lee Bennett Hopkins Poetry Award, The Coretta Scott King Author Honor, and the 2017 Inaugural Pat Conroy Legacy Award. In 2018, he opened the Barbara E. Alexander Memorial Library and Health Clinic in Ghana, as a part of LEAP for Ghana, an international literacy program he co-founded. He is the host and executive producer of *America's Next Great Author,* and the co-showrunner and executive producer of *The Crossover* TV series on Disney+.